"Choung's 'napkin theology' and its 'four-worlds' diagram promise to be for evangelism in the twenty-first century what the 'Four Spiritual Laws' were for the twentieth century."

LEONARD SWEET, AUTHOR OF *THE CHURCH OF THE PERFECT STORM*

"*True Story* reminds us that our news really is good, and helps us communicate that message simply and comprehensively using four simple circles."

DON EVERTS, AUTHOR OF *JESUS WITH DIRTY FEET*

"James Choung provides a blueprint that will challenge the unbeliever, the new believer and the longtime church member to discover the fresh and healing message of the gospel."

SOONG-CHAN RAH, MILTON B. ENGEBRETSON ASSISTANT PROFESSOR OF CHURCH GROWTH AND EVANGELISM, NORTH PARK THEOLOGICAL SEMINARY

"[This] invitation to join Jesus' missional community is both compelling and good news to all who hear it."

TERRY ERICKSON, NATIONAL DIRECTOR OF EVANGELISM, INTERVARSITY CHRISTIAN FELLOWSHIP

"Choung's rethinking and recrafting of Christ's timeless call is exactly what we need today to present the gospel to a new generation of unconvinced people."

KEN FONG, SENIOR PASTOR, EVERGREEN BAPTIST CHURCH OF LOS ANGELES

"[*True Story*] does not gloss over sincere and profound questions concerning the content of the gospel and the way it is lived out, but grapples with many issues that arise in the give-and-take of a discussion between friends."

EDDIE GIBBS, AUTHOR OF *CHURCHNEXT* AND *LEADERSHIPNEXT*

"Honestly, I've never been a fan of diagrams, but Choung shares some incredibly simple but profound illustrations that help elucidate the good news in a biblically faithful and culturally relevant manner."

EUGENE CHO, LEAD PASTOR, QUEST CHURCH, SEATTLE

"I highly recommend this book as a fresh articulation and narrative of what is truly the *good* news! It's more than a fire escape . . . it's a revolution of justice, advocacy and radical compassion. I'm in!"

DAVE GIBBONS, FOUNDER AND LEAD PASTOR, NEWSONG CHURCH, AND CVO, XEALOT INC.

"This insightful book offers a way of presenting the good news that fully engages with today's complex postmodern issues and questions simply by refocusing on the original message of the gospel of Jesus our Savior."

PETER T. CHA, ASSOCIATE PROFESSOR OF PASTORAL THEOLOGY, TRINITY EVANGELICAL DIVINITY SCHOOL

"James Choung has recaptured the world-saving, life-transforming message of the gospel. . . . A true-to-life journey of rediscovering the hope of Jesus that answers the most vexing issues of our world."

ALLEN MITSUO WAKABAYASHI, AUTHOR OF *KINGDOM COME*

"Quite different—written as simply as possible, never losing sight of the big story that Jesus Christ is the ultimate. This is a book for today's generation, seeking truth, satisfaction and fulfillment."

MANFRED W. KOHL, VICE PRESIDENT, OVERSEAS COUNCIL INTERNATIONAL

"James Choung's winsome narrative grapples with many questions of faith that seekers and also Christians wrestle with in this postmodern world."

DOUG BIRDSALL, EXECUTIVE CHAIR, LAUSANNE COMMITTEE FOR WORLD EVANGELIZATION

"*True Story* is for anyone serious about communicating the good news of Jesus in a thoughtful, biblical way which leans into—instead of running from—the pressing issues all around us in the secularized, post-Christian culture of the Western world."

SAM METCALF, PRESIDENT, CHURCH RESOURCE MINISTRIES—U.S.

TRUE STORY

A Christianity
Worth Believing In

JAMES CHOUNG

IVP Books

An imprint of InterVarsity Press
Downers Grove, Illinois

InterVarsity Press
P.O. Box 1400, Downers Grove, IL 60515-1426
World Wide Web: www.ivpress.com
E-mail: email@ivpress.com

InterVarsity Press® is the book-publishing division of InterVarsity Christian Fellowship/USA®, a student
movement active on campus at hundreds of universities, colleges and schools of nursing in the United States of
America, and a member movement of the International Fellowship of Evangelical Students. For information
about local and regional activities, write Public Relations Dept., InterVarsity Christian Fellowship/USA, 6400
Schroeder Rd., P.O. Box 7895, Madison, WI 53707-7895, or visit the IVCF website at <www.intervarsity.org>.

All Scripture quotations, unless otherwise indicated, are taken from the Holy Bible, Today's New
International Version™ Copyright © 2001 by International Bible Society. All rights reserved.

Design: Cindy Kiple

Images: napkin note: Stefan Klein/iStockphoto
marker: Olivier Bondeau/iStockphoto
coffee stain: Ian Soper/iStockphoto

ISBN 978-0-8308-3609-3

Printed in the United States of America ∞

Library of Congress Cataloging-in-Publication Data

Choung, James, 1973-
True story: a Christianity worth believing in / James Choung.
    p. cm.
Includes bibliographical references.
ISBN 978-0-8308-3609-3 (pbk.: paper)
1. Conversion—Christianity. 2. Apologetics. 3. Evangelistic work.
I. Title.
BR110.C44 2008
239-dc22

                                                                            2007049470

| P | 18 | 17 | 16 | 15 | 14 | 13 | 12 | 11 | 10 | 9 | 8 | 7 | 6 | 5 | 4 | 3 | 2 |
| Y | 23 | 22 | 21 | 20 | 19 | 18 | 17 | 16 | 15 | 14 | 13 | 12 | 11 | 10 | 09 | 08 |

To Isaiah —

May you do justice,

love mercy,

and walk humbly with our God.

Contents —

Before We Start—

Back in college I started a Bible study with eight friends who didn't follow Jesus. Each week we met in our fraternity's chapter room and studied the Scriptures together. Any question about Jesus or Christianity was fair game, and the conversation floated easily between the outrageous and the sublime. And I'd often have to say, "Sure, *that's* an interesting point, but what does the text say?" We had a good time with lots of laughter, and we always left the heavy wooden sliding door half open in case a fraternity brother wanted to stop by and join in.

One week someone did. During our Bible study I noticed Keith* just outside the chapter room. He leaned back against the wall with his arms crossed and listened to our conversation. I invited him in, but he felt fine where he was. So we continued the study, and I taught that our sins had separated us from God, but Jesus died in our place so that we could have eternal life in heaven. Keith suddenly interrupted us with an edgy voice: "So, you think I'm going to hell?"

All heads turned to Keith, and then to me. I took a deep breath and said, "You don't have to. You have the chance to be in heaven one day. You can accept Jesus into your heart." I honestly thought it was a solid answer. But his face fell and tears started to fall. His voice shook when he asked, "But what if my parents don't become Christians?"

I started to say, "They have a chance too, if they . . ."

But he shot back quickly, "If my parents are going to hell, then I'd

---

*Not his real name.

rather be in hell with my family than be in heaven alone!" As abruptly
as he had entered the conversation, he turned hard and left.

"But . . ."

I wanted to share so much more. Following Jesus is about more than
heaven and hell, or who's in or out. Isn't it? But instead I felt like the
bad guy. The word *evangelism* comes from the Greek word *euangelion*,
which literally means "good news." I wanted to share good news, but
the message clearly didn't feel all that good to Keith. The rest of the
Bible study thought it was a bit harsh too. I had the sinking feeling that
this message might not feel good to many of my friends.

It's easy to be afraid of coming off as irrelevant, offensive, exclu-
sionary and closed-minded when talking about the gospel. And these
days no one wants to be closed-minded. Sharing our faith can feel like
putting ourselves in front of the firing squad of shame and rejection. We
deal with enough of that in everyday life—why add more? It's demo-
tivating: why share a message that will draw scorn and ridicule? We
want to keep our friends, not push them away, right? Ultimately, we
don't really feel like we have good news to share. At least, not to them.
But that makes me wonder if we really have what Jesus taught in the
first place. Because when he taught it, it must've felt like good news.

While I don't want to water down the message just to say what others want to hear, I do want to share what Jesus came to teach. So what
exactly did he teach? What was his central message? Shouldn't we
share that with our friends? If we present a faith that's only concerned
about the eternal destination of a soul after death, then perhaps we've
missed the mark. And if we share a faith that ignores broken relationships and societal injustices, then we've done our Christian faith a dis-
service. Jesus' message is about so much more than most of us realize,
and it seems right to share the good news he came to offer.

When it comes to evangelism, many authors have written about loving God with all our heart, mind, soul and strength and loving others, and how the credibility of our lives connects to sharing our faith. Others have written about practical strategies for sharing our faith, such as servant evangelism or investigative Bible studies. These teachings are good and needed. But I don't need to waste pulp and ink adding to either side.

Instead, I want to address the very message of the gospel and how we communicate it. It's true that many authors have also written books on the message of Jesus—Dallas Willard, N. T. Wright and Brian McLaren, for starters. But they're all the length of, well, books. And sure, we have the chance to offer books to friends who are curious about the faith. But what if a time comes when you're asked about the central message of the faith? Sometimes "Go read this book" sounds more evasive than helpful. Your friends may really want to know from you, because they've seen Jesus most clearly through you.

What you have in your hands is, obviously, also of bookish length. But its purpose is to highlight a gospel-illuminating tool called "the Big Story." This story is a way of sharing the gospel that is, as Einstein said, as "simple as possible, but not simpler," capturing more fully the good news as Jesus taught it while also making it easier to share. Now, I don't believe a diagram will save the world, nor do I even think a diagram is the best way to share our faith. Nevertheless, diagrams are powerful and memorable icons and have a great shaping influence on what we think about as the central message of the faith. And I can't help but wonder if past icons have kept us from fully understanding the gospel.

True Story, therefore, begins with a fictional story to illustrate the questions, struggles, joys and hopes surrounding the gospel. Sharing these ideas in a story keeps us from merely playing intellectual exercises but gives our truths a realistic context in which to roam and explore the grassy land. Stories not only engage our minds, they also cut through the barbed-wired fences of our hearts and rope us in. They beg us to connect with their characters and themes, and they often end up teaching us about ourselves. It makes sense that Jesus used stories to teach.

At the story's conclusion, a briefer section follows to explain the Big Story diagram and its application in more detail. Through both sections, I hope that even if we disagree on a few smaller theological points, we'll ultimately agree that we need a gospel that incorporates our personal transformation, our need for community and our call to love our neighbors in the world—one that more fully reflects the kingdom of God. Because what we share with our friends reflects what we believe is the central message of the Christian faith.

St. Peter says in 1 Peter 3:15 that Christians should "always be prepared to give an answer to everyone who asks you to give the reason for the hope that you have." So when the occasion arises, my hope is that this book will provide us a simple tool to share the hope that we have— one worth believing in.

Once Upon a Time—

Art thou for something rare and profitable?

Wouldst thou see a truth within a fable?

JOHN BUNYAN, *THE PILGRIM'S PROGRESS*

A Crisis of Faith

ALTAR

The drizzle sprayed lightly on the windshield as Caleb drove home. The day had been tough, so he turned off the music to think more clearly. He could now hear the sound of rain gently hitting the roof of the car, the baritone rhythm of the wiper blades, and the occasional swish of rubber running over wet asphalt.

His slim frame let out a long sigh. Though he was only a sophomore at the University of Washington, his life seemed a total failure. His microbiology midterm score was low enough to put his medical school future on the altar.

Kill it mercifully, he thought as he wrung the steering wheel.

Med school wasn't even his idea. He pictured his dad crossing his arms and his mom shooting deadly looks if he ever told them he didn't want to go. It sent a chill down his back.

"Asian parents," he sighed. He quickly decided not to tell them about his midterm, at least not tonight.

He made his way down Forty-Fifth Street, approaching the right turn where he would head north on I-5. As he merged onto the freeway, he didn't pay attention to the small streaks his aging wiper blades left on the windshield. Instead, his mind was on something else entirely.

BENTO

Earlier that day Caleb and Anna had been having a late lunch over a couple of teriyaki-chicken bentos at Naoko's. The lunch crowd had already thinned out, leaving only three other customers in the restaurant, so they were able to sit near the window.

Caleb had met Anna Hughes in Psych 202—biopsychology—last quarter when they'd been assigned to the same group project. They became good friends. Today, she wore a secondhand-store jacket over a black T-shirt that said, "Save Darfur." And he couldn't help noticing the way her blonde hair rested on her shoulders. But he didn't want to stare, so he instinctively looked down at the pieces of tofu and seaweed floating in his bowl of miso soup.

After a sip of the soup, Caleb looked up to see her blue eyes staring hard at him. She had a habit of doing this, especially when she wanted to grab his attention from the mire of his own thoughts—and it always unnerved him. He'd been silently repeating his mantra of the afternoon: *No, this isn't a date. We're just friends.*

He coughed, blushed a bit and put the soup back on the table. He stared for a moment at the billowing clouds of miso turning in his bowl. She didn't seem to care.

"What's up?" he said, trying to be nonchalant.

"I saw something today that totally bugged me," she said. "I was in Red Square on my way to class. Did you know there was a Pride rally today? It was wet out there, but lots of people still came out. And it was crazy—costumes, makeup, all of that. But what bugged me was the group of people on the sidelines. They shouted and screamed, yelling and saying nasty things. They held signs that said, 'God hates fags' or 'AIDS is God's curse.' They started chanting, 'Burn in hell! Burn in hell!' They were Christians! And they were angry."

"But—" started Caleb, lifting his hands in protest.

"I know, I know," she said. "Not all Christians are like that. Relax, will you? I'm not talking about you. But come on: what good is Christianity if it makes people like that? What good is any religion if it just makes them angry, critical and narrow-minded?"

He tried to cut in again. "I'm not finished," she said. She spoke slowly now. "It finally hit me. They reminded me of the church I used to go to. You know, I used to go all the time before college, but I haven't been back since. Maybe they're not out there with picket signs yelling at gays and lesbians. But they were pretty critical. The youth pastor always made me feel totally guilty. Every week I had to sit and listen to him pick at every tiny fault I had. I couldn't have any fun—I couldn't even breathe. Either I listened to the wrong radio stations, asked the wrong questions, wore the wrong clothes or dated the wrong boyfriend. They even tried to cast a demon out of me—I think they called him 'Bob.'"

Caleb smiled at that one.

"I couldn't get it right the way you did," Anna said, now with more gravity. "God wanted it perfect, and he was always looking down at me, hoping I'd be better but knowing I never would be. He was always right—I was always wrong. It's like he had a report card, and I always came out below the curve. I can't help but think he's bummed out, disappointed and pissed off with me. And isn't God looking down at the Pride rally too? Isn't he just as critical, shaking his head and writing them off too?" She pointed at Caleb accusingly.

Her intensity carried her like a river's current. "Yeah, he probably is. Just like everyone at church. Just like the people at the Pride rally. Just like my dad. He was a deacon at our church, and he . . ." Anna's voice trailed off and she fixed her gaze over Caleb's shoulder, watching the cars pass by outside the restaurant window.

Caleb wondered what she was looking at. He waited for her to say something else. She didn't, so he glanced around the room, looking for anything to distract him from the awkward silence. He couldn't figure out what was going on. He heard a few more cars swoosh by on the wet concrete. Then he shifted in his chair, and the throbbing pulse in his ears grew louder and louder.

With a tear falling and her teeth clenched, Anna broke the silence. "Christianity's just another screwed-up religion! Look at what Christians do: they guzzle gas with their SUVs, join the NRA, picket abortion centers, bomb other countries and spend, spend, spend at the mall, right? They only care about themselves. Seriously, what has Christianity done for us—or the world for that matter? They're just a bunch of hypocrites, that's what I think! Are they good for anything?" At the word *good*, her hands hit the table with a thud that drew the glance of the other customers.

She glared at Caleb while wiping away tears, waiting for a reply. Long seconds ticked away. He scrambled back into his mind, trying to find something that would sound great, hoping that something— anything—would give him the right words to cool off the white heat of anger. But he found none. He wished he could transform into an ostrich and stick his head in the sand. He furrowed his brow even further. He exhaled hard and shrugged his shoulders, saying the only truthful thing he could at that time.

"I don't know," he said, shaking his head. "I just don't know."

SCRIPT

Caleb turned onto the freeway, where a sea of blinking brake lights lit up the wet concrete like a Christmas tree. He groaned: after fifteen minutes he'd only reached the Lake City Way exit, and he knew that it would be a long commute home. So he had time to let his words to Anna echo loudly in his mind: "I just don't know." After a moment, his face flushed and sweat started to collect around his neck. *I'm a moron.* Keeping one hand on the wheel, he took off his fleece and opened the vent to let some cool air in.

He recalled his pastor's challenge, to "do the work of an evangelist." If that charge had come from anyone else, Caleb wouldn't be feeling the angst he was right now. But Jeff Corbin had everyone's respect: not only was he a great speaker, he'd also grown his ministry from twenty to about two hundred in the last four years. And he believed in Caleb; he'd given him a chance to lead worship at Experience, the college ministry at University Community Church. They spent a lot of time together, and Caleb felt Pastor Jeff's care and concern deeply. Caleb didn't want to let him down.

Pastor Jeff had said that no leader at Experience was exempt from this charge. He reminded them that in the Bible, Timothy received the charge even though he had a hard time speaking up—even though he wasn't the "evangelistic" type. Caleb led worship at Experience, which meant he held the title of *leader,* but he couldn't even get the band to sound right, much less share the faith with his friends.

I'm no evangelist. Caleb had earnestly tried to share his faith with his high school buddies, and he'd continued to do so when he lived in the dorms his freshman year. Some friends had even started coming to Experience—their first forays into a religious community—because of his efforts.

Still, being called an "evangelist" conjured up images of Brother Jeb, who wore sandwich billboards depicting silhouetted mobs burning in red-hot hellfire. Brother Jeb would storm through UW's Red Square like a tornado, squashing any ounce of interest an observer might have about Christianity with his fist-raised condemnations against atheists, homosexuals, liberals, tree-huggers, hecklers and anyone else who dared stand in his path.

I know, I know. Caleb could almost hear Pastor Jeff's voice asserting that he wasn't asking Caleb to be Brother Jeb. He just wanted him to share his faith with his friends. It wasn't an unreasonable request: didn't Jesus want him to do that as well? Yet Caleb felt like Brother Jeb when his friends asked, "What about those people who have never heard about Jesus? Are they going to hell?"

He usually recited the answers he had been taught. But he felt like an actor in a bad B-movie who still faithfully delivered his lines. Whenever someone said Christians were hypocrites, he couldn't help but feel a twinge of sympathy for their point of view.

Suddenly a Grand Cherokee swerved into his lane, barely missing his front bumper. He leaned on the horn far longer than needed to give the warning.

I could win an Oscar.

VALUES

He tailed the Cherokee until his car crawled past the Northgate Mall. Then he gave up the chase and allowed his heart rate to lower back to normal. His thoughts went back to Anna's question in the restaurant: are Christians really good for anything?

Shifting in his seat, he tried to answer the question as best he could, mentally compiling a list of Christian values: Christians should become more like Jesus. Yes, and they should have a vibrant, authentic relationship with God—talking to God, hearing from God, acting on what they'd heard. Christians should also witness about their faith to their friends, both here and abroad. They shouldn't be hermits— they should love each other, interacting as a community. Christians should love the poor and fight for justice. And didn't the call of Jesus propel them to the forefront of racial healing, of bridge-building between Hutu and Tutsi, Serb and Croat, Arab and Jew? And what about spending less on their own material possessions so they could give more away? Shouldn't they try to make this world a better place? Yes, Jesus would want this for all of his followers, right? It seemed like the kind of community that Jesus envisioned.

The traffic slowed even further—a pedestrian would have outpaced his car. But by now Caleb didn't care. His eyes glowed with new energy as he continued to flesh out his vision. *Christians like this could change the world!* he thought, tapping the steering wheel like Thumper after seeing Bambi bounce into the forest glen.

But Christians didn't usually look like this, he thought. Some who had an inkling of being called to this lifestyle chose to ignore it because of the inconvenience and difficulty. Like Hollywood stars who crave both publicity and privacy, these Christians wanted both the security of faith and the dream of prosperity and prestige—and they questioned neither. Others didn't know—they were well-meaning Christians who'd never been taught to live this way. Did the gospel even tell them to live this way? The gospel was only about life *after* death, right? No Christian needed to live this way. They were all getting into heaven anyway, right?

GARBAGE

Caleb looked back and checked his blind spot. As he changed lanes he had a surprising thought: *Maybe that's why Christians are so focused on converting people. It's only about heaven, right?* But that couldn't be . . .

His memories of Manila popped up and shouted that it couldn't be. Last summer he'd found himself with a group of college students from all over the country, but mostly from San Diego. He'd expected their tans, their flip-flops and their constant use of the word *dude*, but they'd surprised him with their lack of cynicism and utter openness to God. Before they left for Manila they read articles together about injustices in the world—between men and women, black and white, rich and poor, America and the rest of the world. They also studied Old Testament prophets like Amos and Isaiah, who described God's great compassion for the poor and oppressed. It had been like getting a new pair of glasses: he could see more clearly but his head started to hurt with all the new ideas and implications.

Living in Manila for six weeks with the urban poor had rent his heart wide open. His team had slept in the slums, shantytowns built on top of smoldering garbage mountains. The sour stench never went away, but after the first few nights the mini-explosions—set off by the buildup of methane gas under the decomposing trash—no longer surprised him. He slept in a small shack of corrugated metal built so precariously that he was afraid to lean against it for fear of pushing the whole thing into the polluted river behind them. The slum's residents collected recyclables and other garbage and sold it to middlemen for pennies a day. Yet they survived. He'd never seen anything like this. And often he wondered what God could do in a place like this. Was he even here? Caleb wasn't in Seattle anymore, and he wondered if he could click his heels three times and return home.

One morning the neighborhood had been eerily quiet. Blood was splattered across the wall of one of the shacks, and the children were sitting in front of it in a daze. This would've been a bad horror movie in the making if it weren't so real.

This can't be good, he thought.

Then the news came: a teenager had been knifed to death the night before in a tussle with drug dealers. The team started to pray, more intensely than Caleb had ever prayed before. Some villagers wondered what they were doing, especially when they put their hands on the children to bless them and pray for their protection. But others joined in. The villagers prayed in Tagalog, and though Caleb didn't comprehend their spoken language, he understood their hearts. Their prayers quilted them into one. And as they held hands in that moment, the entire team recognized that even here in the slums there was hope for a broken world. Because God was there. In turn God was pouring into them a love for people who were nothing like their highly educated yet apathetic American peers.

Later, back in the States, Pastor Jeff asked the new leaders at Experience to share about their summers. Caleb couldn't help but gush over the things that he had learned, particularly that God was a God of peace and justice and had a special place in his heart for the poor. Caleb shared with tears in his eyes about how Experience could start supporting the poor overseas, how they could hold prayer meetings for the people that he had met and fallen in love with. He stood up and pleaded with them to make more space in their hearts and schedules for this. Then he sat down.

"That's awesome, bro!" Pastor Jeff said. "It's great to see what God's doing in your life! And those are great ideas. Let's think about how we can do some of those things. So how many got saved?"

"Um, we didn't really get that far. I mean, I guess we were just 'sowing seeds.'"

"Okay, that's a good start," he said, trying not to sound disappointed. Then he turned back to the rest of the students, "So, what else happened this summer?"

Four other students shared. Then Lisa raised her hand and said, "I felt God leading me to pray for my best friend Janet every day this summer. I thought, 'How can we be best friends if we don't even talk about Jesus?' I was always afraid to bring him up. But we were just hanging out one day and I felt like I had to share about my faith. I told her about Jesus and why he's important to me. I wanted my best friend to know what he'd done in my life. She listened, like *really* listened. So I invited her to come to church with me, and she's been coming to Experience for the past month. She's not a Christian yet, but I think she's really close. Isn't that awesome? Would you guys pray for her?"

"That's incredible!" Pastor Jeff said. "Did you hear Lisa's story? Did you see what she did? And did you see what God did? That's what we need to be about here at Experience. I've been praying all summer about the upcoming year, and we need to be focused. This year we need to do what Lisa did. This year needs to be about evangelism."

Jeff beamed, but Caleb slumped in his chair and buried his head in his hands.

BRIDGE

The traffic started to ease up and Caleb's thoughts sped ahead of him.

Before Manila, Caleb had always gone to Pastor Jeff for advice on ministry, faith and girls—not necessarily in that order. Since Manila, however, Caleb had increasingly withdrawn. To him, Pastor Jeff seemed increasingly concerned only about building the Experience empire.

Although Caleb knew this critique was a bit unfair, something was starting to click on this drive home. For Pastor Jeff it was all about heaven. If someone wasn't secured a place in heaven, then all efforts should be marshaled to help people get in, right? The mantra was, "We should try to get as many people as possible to Experience so they can hear the gospel and be saved." Serving the poor in Manila, no matter how worthy a cause, didn't come anywhere close to saving a soul.

This is crazy. Is there a possibility that we Christians aren't living out our faith not despite—but precisely because of *—what we've been taught?*

The windshield had clouded up, so Caleb hit the defrost button. As the fog slowly disappeared, his mind still scrambled for clarity.

Okay, start at the beginning. What's the gospel? He pictured the bridge diagram that Pastor Jeff had taught him:

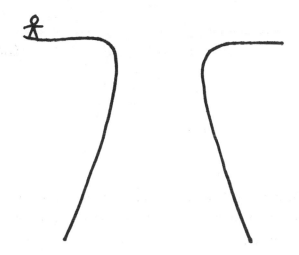

When a person sinned—by lustfully looking at a hot girl or breaking curfew and thereby disobeying his parents—God became furious with him. God couldn't stand sin; he was too perfect to have sin anywhere near him. So in his wrath he punished the sinner for eternity. The person was, therefore, separated from God. "For the wages of sin is death."

Jesus, God's Son, Caleb went on thinking, suffered the cruelest death ever invented by humankind—crucifixion. As proof that God had power over sin and death, God raised Jesus back to life. Through the ultimate act of sacrifice and forgiveness, people could now be with God forever; Jesus died to pay for their sins so they could go to heaven when they died. All they had to do was accept what Jesus had done and then enjoy paradise forever. Caleb pictured in his mind how a person could cross over the bridge of Jesus to meet God on the other side:

Jesus, innocent of any wrongdoing, took that person's punishment on himself. As in an exchange of hostages, Jesus died instead of the prisoner.

"His life for mine," Caleb said aloud. "I'm forgiven." Pastor Jeff would've been proud.

Forgiveness was Christianity's unique claim in the market of world religions, and it defended Caleb from the guerilla warfare of self-condemnation that often sent multiple sorties into his head and heart. Whenever he felt himself hating his parents for their unfair expectations or succumbed to Internet pornography, he would wallow in his shame.

But at some point he would find himself able to ask God for forgiveness. He would remind himself that Jesus had paid for his sins and that God still loved him. Then the truth would sink in: mercy triumphs over judgment. No condemnation—he was guilt- and shame-free.

Caleb could rest knowing he couldn't do anything to make God love him less or more. He was saved not by works but by God's grace. He needed only to accept the truth of what Jesus had already done. He needed only to believe and enjoy God's embrace. Through Jesus his relationship with God was restored. And it was God's mercy that extended this wonderfully unfair forgiveness to him so that in turn he could forgive others. Sometimes he had trouble trusting this message, but in the end he needed it. *Where would I be without the gospel? This is good news, right?*

The red lights of the car in front of him flashed on, and its rear bumper kicked up suddenly. He hit his brakes hard, avoiding the collision.

I should pay more attention to the road.

RIVER

But his mind ignored the brake lights and continued down the same road. If people only needed to accept this truth to be saved, then could a Christian go to heaven believing in Jesus yet hating Arabs? Could Christians accept what Jesus had done for them and still buy large houses and vacation homes, drive Benzes, jet-set to Monaco, and dine on prime filet and Dom Perignon while giving nothing to people who foraged in a garbage dump to put food on the table? If they could afford it, Western Christians tended to go for the good life. So would they go to heaven? Caleb suddenly heard the voice of Martin Luther King Jr. thundering in his head, quoting Amos: "Let justice roll on like a river, righteousness like a never-failing stream!"

Where were these streams and rivers in the church? With the gospel of the bridge illustration, Christians didn't need to share their faith with others, stand up for the oppressed, become more like Jesus, love people of other cultures and ethnicities, take care of the environment or be concerned about the poor at all. If they just believed, they'd be in heaven, right? And they could still claim to have a relationship with Jesus. Everything else was just extra credit.

Caleb thought about Jesus' story of the sheep and the goats—those who didn't feed the hungry, offer a drink to the thirsty, welcome the stranger, clothe the naked, care for the sick or visit the prisoner suffered eternal punishment. But the gospel also seemed to say that to end up in paradise, you just needed to believe Jesus died for your sins—even if nothing in your life reflected his teachings.

Caleb gripped the steering wheel hard, his knuckles turning white. He didn't notice that he was clenching his jaw. Would Christians who didn't love their neighbor get into heaven? If he were pressed into a theological corner and asked to fight, he'd have to drop his hands and surrender. The answer according to the gospel he'd been taught was "yes." Their punishment had been paid. No lives needed to change. Nothing else needed to happen. Believe in your mind; confess with your lips; accept the truth in your heart—and Jesus would make sure you got into heaven. Such a faith had nothing to do with life here and now but only the life to come. Caleb didn't need to try to change the world or make it a better place. He could just wait—while keeping his personal relationship with Jesus intact—for paradise after death.

Where is the abundant life Jesus promised in that? Caleb was losing feeling in his fingertips, and the assault of questions didn't let up. What did this gospel have to do with living out faith today? What was faith supposed to look like? What *was* faith? What was the gospel? Was this truth? Or were the last twenty years of his spiritual life a farce? If he could question the central message of his faith, he could question anything. Everything was suspect.

I can't believe I'm thinking this way. Caleb's heart pounded heavily. But his thoughts continued down their path. When he considered Pastor Jeff's challenges and strategies, evangelism seemed like just another way for Christians to force their superiority on others, arrogantly proclaiming their lock on the truth. *How do we proclaim one objective truth in a world that sees many paths to God? We may have the truth, but what's the good in that? What good news are we bringing to a suffering world? Do we even have good news to share?*

Caleb knew the Bible was full of great news, but the gospel he'd been taught seemed to leave out all the revelations he'd learned in Manila: that God loves the poor, that he comforts the suffering, that he reconciles people to one another and heals the sick. This should have felt like a cure for AIDS—it was good news for all people, whether they had AIDS or not. But his gospel didn't talk about these things. It simply offered people an escape from the world's troubles through death into a life with God. It didn't seem to care about a suffering world. So Christians didn't care about a suffering world. In fact, they seemed like the most selfish pigs on the planet! Maybe Anna was right.

Blood rushed to Caleb's face. He slammed his fist down hard on the dashboard and shouted, "This is not good news!" His eyes started to water. And with the drizzle, it was as if God's tears were joining his. His thoughts finally quieted, and the only sound was the *whump-whump* of the wiper blades.

SEARCH

Caleb finally parked his car and walked through his front door, joining his parents for a quiet dinner before going up to his room to work on his organic chemistry problems. But he couldn't will himself to care about the difference between a ketone and an aldehyde. He closed the textbook, needing someone to talk to about his questions.

He picked up his phone and called Dave Morrison, who played bass behind him on the worship team. Dave was one of his best friends, and he had to let him know what was on his mind.

"I'm crazy, right?" asked Caleb.

"Yup. Certified," Dave answered in his low, laid-back voice.

"I'm being serious, man."

"Okay. I dunno . . . have you prayed about it?"

"Not really," Caleb replied. "I'm still processing."

"Still, maybe you should. What about Pastor Jeff?"

"I want to talk to him," Caleb said, grimacing. "But things don't seem right between us these days. I don't know if he'll understand."

"Hmm. How about Professor Jones? Remember she said that we could come to her with any question? It seems like she might have wrestled through this stuff."

Shalandra Jones was an ethnic studies professor who taught classes on religion and race, and they both had taken her class last quarter. She definitely cared about larger issues in the world. That was clear from her classes. She had also spoken at Experience about the need for active reconciliation between people of different ethnicities and cultures and had offered a standing invitation for people to come see her during her office hours. But were her views biblical? Caleb just didn't know. Still, it was a place to start.

"That's not a bad idea," said Caleb. "I'll look her up. Thanks."

"I'll be praying for you. And I'll remind Tom to pray too. Hey, so what's going on with you and Anna these days?"

Caleb grinned sheepishly and was glad Dave couldn't see it. "I'll tell you about it tomorrow," said Caleb. "I promise."

"Okay, but don't leave me hangin' too long."

Caleb went straight to his computer. He searched for "Shalandra Jones" on the Internet, and the results led him to the UW website. Her office hours were listed on her faculty bio page. Perfect. He could meet her tomorrow afternoon.

Then he asked God for guidance. *Lord, help me . . .*

EMBRACE

In the morning Caleb drove to school in yet another day of drizzle. But today something was pushing him through the rain. Or perhaps it was pulling, leading him through traffic until he parked in the underground lot. After his classes, it ushered him eastward across campus to Padelford Hall. It shepherded him to the black-paneled directory and through the long wait for the elevator to a fifth-floor office in the American Ethnic Studies department.

The door was wide open. It was a small room, and Professor Jones had her back to him; she was leaning back in her chair staring out through the tall windows. Books filled the shelves lining every wall, and papers were piled high on the cherry desk. Behind Professor Jones a colorful Kenyan tapestry hung over a burgundy leather chair. She kept the fluorescent lights off, and the glow from a tall floor lamp and a desk lamp gave a warm touch to an already-inviting room.

Caleb hadn't said a word, but Professor Jones swiveled around anyway. She smiled broadly. "Can I help you?" she asked.

He smiled back. "Um . . . I was wondering if you had some time to talk?"

"Sure, that's why I'm here," she said. She spoke clearly and deliberately, like someone who'd been teaching a long time. She stood up to greet him, appearing even taller than she was due to her slender frame and heeled shoes. Her hair was dark and natural: tightly curled and cropped short. Her black-framed glasses and professional gray suit gave her an air of authority and credibility. Otherwise she might have looked quite young—like a student herself.

"Hi, professor. I'm—"

"Caleb, right? I remember you." She stepped forward and wrapped him in a strong hug. For a split second he squirmed. But quickly a rush of warmth flowed into him and dispelled the drizzle's chill. When she let go, he realized that his neck and shoulders had been tensed for a long time. He took a deep breath and let his body relax. He felt like he'd roamed through a dense, overgrown jungle and finally found a wide path; he didn't know where it would end up, but at least it went somewhere.

"Hang up your coat and have a seat." She motioned to the chair. He sat down and sank into its plush comfort.

"What can I do for you?" she asked as she sat down.

"Professor, I thought you might be able to help me," he started. Then a torrent of words came tumbling out: he described his struggles with his faith, his questions, his frustrations, his concerns—everything he'd been wrestling with. She listened attentively, nodding and saying, "Hmm" at all the right places. When he finally stopped, she smiled. Then she began to talk.

PART ONE

Designed for Good

PILGRIM

Caleb leaned against a pillar, watching Gore-Tex-clad students stream in and out of Odegaard Library. He could feel the coolness of the pillar through his fleece jacket and jeans, and his arms were crossed to keep in the heat. But he was glad to be outside: on a rainy day, the library got stuffy and smelled like damp running shoes. It was great to catch some fresh air.

Besides, he would rather have pushed pins under his fingernails than write his lab report right now. So he took his time, sheltered by the library's protruding second floor, and watched the drizzle wax the brick floor of Red Square into a brilliant shine.

Over a year had passed since that first meeting with Professor Jones, and Caleb was now a junior. He remembered how she had listened patiently while he poured out his soul that day. He'd hoped that she would be able to provide something—anything—to start him in the right direction. He'd been groping about in a dark room, reaching for something solid to orient himself. Even if he found it, he didn't know if he'd be able to stand on his own. But at least it would give him a chance to rest.

She'd said only six words, and he'd clutched at them immediately: "Caleb, you're asking the right questions."

No one had ever validated his questions before. Some of his Christian friends had thought he was becoming liberal—their replacement word for "heretic." His irreligious friends couldn't figure out what the big deal was. Everyone knew he was wrestling through his faith, but no one knew how to help him. And he had no idea how to begin. Professor Jones had said it was okay—even good—to search, to question, to grope, to grieve, to discover. The search itself was a valid one. So instead of feeling like a runaway, he'd begun to feel like a pilgrim.

He had met with Professor Jones every week for couple of months, and then it tapered off to once every two or three weeks. During this time he felt like he'd pulled up the only anchor he'd ever known, and the ship of his faith was floating away from port. He didn't know if he'd ever find another place to dock, another safe harbor for shelter, but he was thankful that at least Professor Jones was there to help him navigate the choppy waters.

Caleb's parents, on the other hand, wanted him to turn in his ticket for a refund. His grades were suffering—particularly in the sciences—and it was clear to them that his ambitions were fierce but impractical. They had given up the medical school dream, but they still wanted him to major in something that would get him a "good job"—perhaps law or engineering. He was looking into ethnic studies instead—clearly not what his parents were hoping for. A switch now would mean he'd be in college for a total of five years, and they weren't thrilled about that. Neither was Caleb, for that matter.

However, despite all the uncertainty surrounding his future, Caleb was fretting more right now about what he was going to do in the next few moments.

SHUFFLE

Caleb inhaled and exhaled slowly, waiting zenlike for an answer. All he heard was drizzle bouncing off the pavement. It sounded like soft, muted radio static.

Fitting. His own mind was receiving signals none too clearly. Anna was inside the library, sitting with her laptop at a study cubicle covered with piles of books and articles. She was writing a paper on the positive and negative effects of globalization on the world's poorest countries, and she was having a hard time coming up with any positives. Caleb wanted to share some of his new revelations about faith with her. But he didn't know how to start.

He pulled out his phone and called Dave, hoping to get some advice. No answer. He hung up without leaving a message, then called Tom. No luck there either. Great. He typed a text message and sent it to both of them: *thinking about talking to anna about j. what do u think?*

Caleb and Anna had engaged in plenty of conversations about religion before. But when Anna got angry or intense—it was often hard for him to tell the difference—he wanted to find the nearest bomb shelter and close the hatch tight. Exasperatingly, she'd just shrug her shoulders. To her they were just having a conversation. They hadn't talked about faith for a while. *It'll be weird to bring it up again, won't it?* he thought. He shuffled his feet back and forth, his thoughts at war with each other.

It didn't help his courage to remember that although his interactions with the professor had been healing, other conversations hadn't gone as well.

STATIC

"Are you questioning the gospel?" Pastor Jeff had asked. He'd smoothed the wrinkles out of his striped button-down and sat up straighter in his chair. He might've run his fingers through his hair if it hadn't been so carefully styled. He stared straight into Caleb's eyes with concern: he'd loved and invested in Caleb too much to let him continue with doctrinal misunderstandings.

This was four months ago. Caleb had felt obligated to make an appointment with him, to let him know about everything he'd been learning. So they were in Pastor Jeff's second-floor office, and they both held Styrofoam cups of office-brewed coffee.

Up to this point the conversation had been friendly. But as Caleb finished describing his theological journey, the room felt as cool as the drizzle outside. As they talked, Caleb felt the off-white walls of the windowless office closing in on him. The folding chair he was sitting in was nowhere as comfortable as the leather one in Professor Jones's office.

"Well, yes," Caleb started to say, until he saw his pastor's brow furrow. "I mean no . . . well, not really, but sort of."

"Bro, the gospel is essential," Jeff said as he tapped his finger on his Bible. "If we can't believe this, then what do we have? If Jesus

didn't die to pay for our sins, then what can we believe in? It's the core
of our faith."

"I know, but—what if we don't have the right gospel? I mean, the
complete picture."

"What do you mean?" Jeff leaned forward on his desk, his forehead
still creased.

"What if we've settled?" asked Caleb, shifting to the edge of his
seat. "What if Jesus did more than we think? What if his message was
more than just dying to pay the penalty of our sins so we can get into
heaven when we die? What if he was saying that we're supposed to live
a certain kind of life, and do good deeds, and . . ."

"Bro, you're starting to get into works-righteousness here," Jeff's
voice was becoming agitated. "We're saved by grace, through faith and
not by works, so that no one can boast. We can't earn our salvation—
it's all from God's mercy. Are you saying that we need to earn our way
into heaven?"

"No, I'm not saying that at all. But what are we saved *for?* Aren't
we also supposed to care for the poor? How does that fit into the gospel? Aren't we supposed to bring reconciliation and justice between
people of different cultures? Or between men and women? Is everything
besides going to heaven extra credit? Is faith only about getting in after
we die? I mean, if Jesus died only for our sins, then we don't have to
care about social justice at all. Stuff like the genocide in Sudan or im-
migration laws in this country shouldn't concern us, right?"

"That sounds like a social gospel."

"But doesn't Jesus want us to be a part of this?" Caleb's voice was
getting edgier too. "According to what you're saying, we don't even
have to become more like Jesus. As long as we believe—"

"Yes—I mean, no, that's not it. It's not like that at all."

"But what the gospel says is—"

"What the gospel says is that Jesus died to pay for our sins. You remember the bridge diagram, right? Our sins separate us from God, and—"

"Yeah, but I don't think that's the whole gospel anymore."

The fluorescent lights buzzed loudly in the ensuing silence. Jeff's master of divinity degree seemed to frown down from its perch on the wall, and Caleb's gaze dropped to his shoes so he didn't have to meet Jeff's wide, shocked eyes. Eventually Jeff shook his head and his face relaxed into a sympathetic look.

"I'll be praying for you," he sighed. "I'm here for you, bro. Let me know whatever you need. Really—I'll be praying for you."

Caleb left the office. After he walked out through the church's front doors, he stopped under the archway and rubbed his temples. He was surprised to find himself shaking. *Am I crazy?*

Jeff was his mentor and friend, and he had relied on his support and encouragement over the past couple of years. It had sustained him. *But . . . he doesn't understand me anymore.* It wasn't safe for him to bring up questions. Emptiness echoed in him like a late-night leaky faucet. His chest tightened. His eyes stung. He bowed his head and shuffled slowly through the drizzle to his parked car.

Back in his office, Jeff reclined in his office chair with his hands tucked behind his head. He let out another long sigh. *Please let it be a phase.* He wasn't going to pull Caleb from the worship team: he didn't have many other options for worship leaders, and Caleb wasn't saying anything crazy from the front of the church or during leadership meetings. Jeff wished he could help in some way. *I wish I had just listened,* he thought. *That probably would've been more helpful.*

But Caleb *was* questioning some of the basics of the Christian faith. Where would he end up in his thinking? Was the professor teaching him the right things? She seemed like a great person, but from what he remembered from her sermon at Experience, she was also on the liberal side. On the other hand, Caleb did bring up some good points: of course we're supposed to love the poor. Jesus did. But was it essential or nonessential? Was it part of the gospel? It didn't seem that way, but . . .

Jeff shook his head vigorously, as if waking from a disturbing dream. He wanted to study this more, especially for Caleb's sake, and he'd jotted down Caleb's book suggestions. But he honestly didn't know when he could get to them: the school year had just started, and it was one of the busiest times of the year.

As he turned back to his desk, Jeff couldn't help but think that Caleb shouldn't be hanging out so much with Anna either.

MOON

Caleb decided he should go back into "Odie" and see what Anna was up to. As he turned toward the library entrance, he felt something sudden and sharp—like a pickup truck was yanking on the other end of a tug-of-war rope in his soul. That got his attention. *Now's the time,* he realized.

He paused and examined his instincts. Perhaps he just didn't want to study and was looking for an excuse. Perhaps he'd had too much caffeine and it was making his heart beat more strongly. But he felt that pull again—actually, it was more like a shove—and he knew he was supposed to talk with Anna about his faith. He needed to. If it was awkward, so be it. Not to do it would make him feel like he'd just slapped his dad.

"Lord, have mercy," he muttered as he went inside.

He found Anna at her cubicle and tapped her on her shoulder. She pulled out her white earphones.

"Anna, I'm done," he said. "Wanna grab some coffee?"

"Sure. Globalization sucks anyway."

They loaded up their bags, left the library and headed for the coffee shop. The rain was letting up, but the city was still swaddled in a blanket of gray. It wasn't a short walk—six long blocks in all. But for Caleb, de Lune was worth it.

The café was a spacious loft with a small, open balcony overlooking the first floor. Its plush yet well-worn velvet couches, wooden coffee tables and armchairs dotted the oft-trodden hardwood floors, welcoming students to take a break from their worries. But the best part of de Lune was the ceiling, where soft spotlights highlighted a hand-painted reproduction of van Gogh's *Starry Night*. If you looked more closely at the mural's blurry moon, you'd see a simple smiley face painted right on top of it, and Caleb often smiled back. He loved this place. Plus, it sold fair-trade coffee, which assuaged Anna's conscience.

The balcony was full, so after getting some coffee, they found a pair of maroon armchairs on the ground floor with a great view of University Avenue, what the locals call "the Ave." John Mayer was playing over the speakers as they sat down, and the orange glow from the table lamps only made Anna look cuter. *She's not a believer,* he reminded himself. He took dating seriously—almost as seriously as sin—and he wanted to have faith at the center of any romantic relationship. Still, Caleb had to concentrate harder than usual to start the conversation.

ELEPHANT

"I want to talk to you about something," Caleb said.

"You look serious, Cay." He couldn't remember when she'd started calling him that, but he liked it. "You want to talk about religion again, right?" she said, rolling her eyes but smiling.

"Yeah, but this time it's different," he said. He couldn't figure out how she always knew what was on his mind. "We both grew up in the church, and we've both heard similar messages from our pastors. But I'm beginning to wonder if we've been duped."

She chuckled wryly. But when she saw that Caleb was earnest, her smirk melted away. She cocked her head slightly to one side.

"What do you mean?" she asked.

"Do you know the core message of the Christian faith?" Caleb asked, taking another sip of his coffee.

"Yeah," said Anna. "It's something like: No one's perfect. Cheat on a test or lie to your parents and you go to hell. So you'd better be good." She winked as she wagged her finger like a prim schoolteacher, then stopped for a moment to think.

"Okay," she continued, "God's like a giant parent, demanding a perfect life. Even perfect grades. But we're messed up, and Jesus had to

die to pay for our sins. Totally sounds like cosmic child abuse to me—
beating up on an innocent guy—but there it is. Jesus died in our place,
and that cleared the way for us to go to heaven, right? And we all have
to speak in tongues." She grinned.

"Sure—well, maybe not that last part," he said, flustered.

"Lighten up, Cay." She jabbed him on the shoulder with enough
force to make him wince.

He smiled weakly and took a deep breath: he was taking himself far
too seriously.

"Not bad," he said, rubbing his shoulder. "Not bad for a *yuj*—I
mean, a girl." She brandished her fist again, and he raised his hands in
mock surrender.

"Okay, okay," he said. "But the rest works for me. Now, what if I
said that that wasn't the whole story, that our pastors and our other
teachers missed out on so much more? By calling that story the central
one, they missed the bigger picture, the truer picture—quite possibly
the core of our faith."

"I'm not exactly sure what you mean."

Caleb thought for a moment, then said, "You've probably heard the
old Hindu analogy about four blind men trying to describe an elephant.
One feels the leg and says it's like a tree. Another feels the trunk and
says it's like a hose. A third feels the tail and says it's like a rope. And
the fourth touches the side and says it's like a wall. Each one describes
the same animal—an elephant—in their own way."

"Yeah, I've heard that. So all religions lead to the same truth."

"Well, people have used that story to say that everyone has different
perspectives on essentially the same thing. But I don't think that's right.
Instead of describing the same thing in different ways, I think each person actually has a distortion—an oversimplification—of what's truly
there. The elephant's not a tree. And it's not a wall or a rope either. So,

here's what I'm wondering: what if Christians today have done the same thing? What if we've just touched a tail and tried to make it the whole elephant? What if we've oversimplified the Christian faith and missed much of what Jesus was really trying to teach us?"

"Do you mean to tell me that pastors don't have it right? That Christians aren't even teaching the Christian message right?"

"Well, no. I mean . . . yeah," Caleb fumbled. "It sounds so strong when you put it that way, but I guess so. They mean well. But Christians boil the gospel down to bumper-sticker formulas like 'God loves you and has a plan for your life.' Or 'If you died tonight, where would you spend eternity?' And when we oversimplify it like that, then we only share one side of the story, even if we don't mean to. We miss the big picture."

"That's crazy. How in the world do we know if we have Jesus' message or not?"

"Well, we can check the sources ourselves. No pastor can trump the Bible. So perhaps we just need a bigger picture of what the Christian faith is about from the Bible. I can show you, if you're interested."

Anna's face tensed up, like a leopard's when it's about to pounce on an unsuspecting antelope on Animal Planet. Unfortunately, Caleb was the antelope.

TRUST

"Hold on a minute," Anna said. "The Bible's got lots of problems. How can we trust it? It was written by people—people who were racist and sexist. People who made mistakes and contradicted each other. People who used Jesus for their own purposes. Wasn't it written way after Jesus' lifetime anyway? We can't really know what Jesus said."

Caleb started to feel warm; he could feel sweat beading up near his brow. This was not where he wanted to go with the conversation. He wished he were outside, cooling off in the winter air.

His phone rang, and he saw that Dave was calling back. He turned off the ringer and put the phone back in his pocket. Then he took off his fleece and took a long breath.

"I hear what you're saying. But if we can't trust the New Testament as history, then we can't trust much of any history."

"Are you serious?" said Anna, shaking her head. "There's evidence for history. It's religion that's biased!"

Caleb blinked rapidly. *That was intense.* He took a moment to collect himself, to keep himself from shutting down. Then he rubbed his hands on his jeans and said, "Sure, religion can be biased. But every credible scholar—whether Christian or not—knows that Jesus actually existed and walked on the planet. Even our profs say that. And we've got more evidence and manuscripts for the New Testament than for any other document. If you can't trust it as history, then you can't trust any ancient source of history."

"I don't think we can trust much of anything," she replied, crossing her arms.

"Well, sometimes you do have to trust someone. The problem is, everything we know about the past is based on trust. If we believe any history, then we trust that somebody has reported it to us accurately. Even if we don't trust the government or the media, we have to trust someone to survive. We might not trust our parents, but we usually trust our friends. Or our teachers. We have to trust that someone's telling us the truth. If we trust no one, then we don't know what we know. Because almost everything we know about things we don't experience ourselves is based on what others tell us. So either we trust someone to tell us something, or we don't know much of anything at all."

"All right," she said, a little defensively. "I see what you're saying. But I'm not going to trust everything."

"But can you think of a better historical source about Jesus' life and teachings besides the Bible?"

"Go on. I'll let it slide for now." She didn't have another answer, but she obviously didn't like conceding the point. She looked out through the window and watched the cars pass by.

This isn't going well, Caleb thought, looking down at his feet. He didn't want to win an argument; he just wanted to have a conversation.

He tugged at his collar, letting some air in. De Lune seemed stuffier than usual tonight. The music in the café seemed louder, too, as the sound of crunch guitars blared through the sound system. *Can't they turn that down?* He tried to focus again.

"Okay. Different question. What do you think about Jesus?"

She looked back at him. "Jesus is cool," she replied. "I'm just not sure about God or Christianity."

Caleb was surprised that Anna had a positive view of Jesus. He grabbed his cup of coffee, took down a few more sips than he'd intended and asked God for more help.

"Okay, do you want to know why Jesus came and what he came to teach?"

Anna nodded. She looked a bit suspicious, but he felt permission to continue.

He took another deep breath, then said, "Let me start with this. Tell me about the world. What do you see on the news?"

"Okay, that's easy," she said, and began to list in rapid-fire. "Geno-

cide in Sudan. Americans killing Iraqis and vice versa. Israel and Leb-
anon bombing each other. Suicide bombers everywhere. Tsunamis.
Earthquakes. Hurricanes. Racism. Sexism. Women being raped and
killed. Children starving. North Korea . . ."

"Yup. That's a list. So—would you agree that the world is really
messed up?"

"Sure, but everyone knows that."

GROAN

Caleb's eyes followed a couple walking past the front windows and into the coffee shop, jingling the bell as they entered. But Anna didn't notice the couple or his discomfort. She waited for his response.

His phone sounded an alert: someone left him a text message. He knew it was either from Dave or Tom, but he felt like he should continue.

"Now, Anna, here's the more important question: how does that make you feel?"

"Feel?"

"Yeah, what goes on inside for you when you hear this stuff?"

"Oh, I love it," she said dryly. "It makes me want to throw a huge party—the Genocide Jam, brought to you by KKLL, where killing your neighbor is cool." She gave two thumbs up and a sarcastic wink.

"What the hell do you think I feel?" she continued, seriously. "Angry. And sad. The world shouldn't be this way!"

"But see, that's really interesting. No normal person responds by cheering and jumping up and down, especially if this stuff has happened to someone close to them." Caleb paused, and his voice broke as he

continued. "My cousin was killed by a drunk driver. She was only seventeen. It's not supposed to happen like that."

"I'm sorry, Cay," she said, putting her hand on his arm. "I didn't
know. When did that happen?"

"A few years ago," he said. He'd surprised himself with his strong
emotional reaction. Though the accident had happened a while ago, losing his cousin at such a young age had felt inherently wrong, as if something were out of place.

Caleb took a moment to gather himself and said, "We all ache—
groan—for something more, don't we? You said it perfectly: the world
shouldn't be this way. If that's true, then that should point to something. I mean, our hunger points to something out there that should
satisfy it—food. Our thirst points to something out there that should
satisfy it—water. And our loneliness points to our need for relationships. So, shouldn't there also be something out there to satisfy the
craving for a better world?"

Anna had pulled her hand back. She said, "But a lot of people crave
things that are bad for them—like drugs."

"Sure, but that just proves my point. Bad or good, something out
there exists to satisfy our cravings—otherwise we wouldn't crave it. So
what would satisfy your craving for a better world?"

She looked up for a moment, and a smile crept across her face.
"Justice," she said. He thought she was going to raise her fist in the
air.

At that moment Caleb was thankful for the conversations he'd had
with Professor Jones. "True, but not in the sense of revenge or pay-
back, right?" he said. "More like right living and right relationships
everywhere—what the Hebrew people called *shalom*. We all want it,
deep down. And I think this basic desire for justice points to the exis-
tence of something in this world that should satisfy it. There was once

a world or there will someday be a world that's like that—a just one where there are right relationships all around. In the Christian worldview, as you remember, there was such a place. It was the way the world was at the beginning . . ."

OUTLOOK

After Caleb's first meeting with Professor Jones, he'd gone back to her office the following week. Seattle was enjoying some sun that day, and the golden mid-afternoon glow made the professor's office look like something out of the medieval Book of Kells. He plopped down in what was quickly becoming his favorite chair in the world.

After their greetings, Caleb said, "Okay, you said we'd start from the beginning."

"Right," the professor said. "And it's important to start from the beginning. It sets everything up in how we think about the world—our worldview. A worldview will answer at least four questions: One, why are we here? Two, what's our problem? Three, what's the solution? And four, where are we going? Got it?" Caleb nodded.

"Good," she continued. "All of this informs our meaning and purpose in the world—and everyone has answers they're living by, whether they know it consciously or not. But you need to keep an open mind." She looked at Caleb to see if he agreed.

"Got it, professor," he said.

"And call me Shalandra."

SWING

Shalandra motioned him to move closer to the desk. He leaned forward, his mind like a fly trap ready to capture anything that buzzed by.

"Caleb," she said, "right now you have many questions. Questions are good—but they're like a wrecking ball. Sometimes a house needs to be destroyed because of mold, rust and rot. It's not suitable to live in anymore. So the wrecking ball swings and knocks it all down." She waved her hand to demonstrate the destructive force. "That's hard, because home is home. You grew up there and found comfort and shelter there for many years. The wrecking ball doesn't feel good. It sure didn't for me."

Caleb nodded, feeling understood.

"Now, what's great is that you already have a foundation: Jesus," she continued. "That firm foundation is still there. But the wrecking ball is destroying your framework. You don't have a home—at least not yet," and here she smiled comfortingly. "But now that you've allowed the wrecking ball to do its work, it's time to put up a new frame—something to which you can attach your walls, ceilings and roof. We need to start from the beginning to build a new frame. Did you bring your Bible?"

BLUEPRINT

"Yup," said Caleb. He gave a mental *whew* when he realized they were going to be looking at Scripture.

"Okay, open up to Genesis 1," she said as she reached for her own Bible. "Tell me what you see. What are some repeated words or phrases?"

"Okay," he said as he quickly skimmed the first chapter. "And God said . . ."

"Good," she said. "What does that mean to you?"

"God did it. He made everything with his words."

"Precisely," she said with a broad smile. "God did it. That's important. The biblical author wanted us to know that creation was not by accident or chance. In another creation story from roughly the same time and location as the book of Genesis, a god created the world from the remains of a slain enemy goddess. In this account the world was created out of violence as a cosmic cleanup effort. The creation of the universe was more improvised than designed."

Caleb nodded in agreement. Not only was the biblical account different from the origin myths of ancient cultures, it was also different from what he was learning in the classroom. The idea of the universe being created by design was definitely countercultural, whether back in history or in the present.

Shalandra pulled out a pen and a pad of lined paper. She drew a picture and said, "This was the world in the beginning."

He said, "Nice world."

She laughed. "So the Israelites had a different idea about the beginning of the world. What else do you see?"

PURPOSE

"And it was so. . . . There was evening and morning, the second or third or whatever day. . . . It was good," Caleb said after skimming for a while.

The sky seemed to be following their conversation, for the swelling darkness was signaling the end of day—there was evening, and morning would eventually come. Shalandra's emerald-colored desk lamp softly lit the room now instead of the sun, which in the winter set as early as 4:30 p.m.

"There," she interrupted. "Yes. It was good. If God designed it all on purpose, he also had a purpose for it. Creation was designed for good. God, like an artist who's proud of her work, looked at the world and everything in it and thought it was good stuff. But it wasn't just artistically good. It was designed for good purposes as well—a land of mutual blessing."

"What do you mean? What kind of purposes?"

Shalandra paused to think. Then she took off her silver watch and held it up. "When I say that this is a 'good watch,' what do I mean?"

"It tells good time. I mean, it's accurate."

"And I don't mean that it's good at everything, like fending off lions.

Down Simba!" she said, swinging her watch playfully. "No, it wasn't made to fend off lions—it was meant to keep time. And when it fulfills its purpose to keep time well, it's a good watch. So in the same way, our world was designed with a purpose in mind, and when God calls it good, he means that it's fulfilling its purpose. Make sense?"

Caleb nodded. He knew that creation was designed by God, but he hadn't thought about its purpose before.

"So, what are those purposes? What does Genesis 2:15 say?" she asked.

"The Lord God took the man and put him in the Garden of Eden to work it and take care of it."

"Right. Creation was meant to be a blessing to humans, and they were meant to be a blessing to it as well. We're supposed to take care of the planet. And from Genesis 1:19, we see that the planet is supposed to take care of us as well. It provides for us. We take care of each other. How does that sound?"

"Great," said Caleb. He grinned: she'd just given him a theological reason to care about the environment. As a native Seattleite, of course he recycled. No less was expected in this city.

"Okay, read Genesis 2:18."

He read, "It is not good for man to be alone. I will make a suitable helper for him."

She pointed to the stick figures in the diagram. Caleb winced, knowing Anna would hate this. "Hold on," he said. "The woman is supposed to be a helper—what do you make of that, professor? Isn't that a little sexist?"

"Great question, Caleb," she said. "In Hebrew, the word *helper* is a compound word, meaning both 'to save' and 'to be strong.' It doesn't have the subservient meaning we give it today. It's used twenty-one times in the Old Testament—seventeen times of God, and is he weaker than us? The female helper was meant to save with strength, making her important and powerful. It's only after the Fall that her desire turned toward her husband and that he came to rule over her. It was a part of the curse and not the way things were originally designed. That's why it's important to know how things were originally designed."

Hmm, he thought. *I wonder if Anna would buy this.*

"She's a strength to him. And he affirms her in Genesis 2:23. Not only were creation and humanity meant to bless each other, but people were meant to bless one another too. In Genesis 2:25 they experience an intimacy in which nakedness causes no shame. They were naked not only in terms of clothing, but also with their emotions, experiences and souls—and they had no shame. How does that sound?"

"Really good," said Caleb. Then he grimaced and bit his lip. He hoped the professor wouldn't take that the wrong way. But he really did wish he could live like that—to be himself without shame.

"Good," she replied, tactfully ignoring Caleb's awkward moment. "So first, you have people and creation blessing each other, and second, you have people blessing other people. That's why the stick figures are close together. And third, you have people and God blessing each other." As she said this, she drew a smaller inner circle:

"In Genesis 1:31, God saved his best praise of creation for human beings, saying after he made them that creation was 'very good.' Up until that point it had only been 'good.' He loved the people he'd made and wanted to be with them, and vice versa—and they had no shame before God, as we know from Genesis 2:25. Even in Genesis 3:9, when he knows they've disobeyed him, God calls out to humankind and asks, 'Where are you?' He wanted to be with us, hang out with us. In fact, he designed the world so that he could hang out with us, and we with him. It was meant to be a relationship of mutual blessing. Everything in the world was meant to be based on love, peace and justice. It was a place of blessing for all. All of creation was designed for good."

And she wrote those words on top of the outermost circle:

Designed for good, he thought. Everything was made to be a source of good for everything else: a land of mutual blessing, a people of mutual blessing and a faith of mutual blessing. Yes, all of it was designed for the purpose of bringing good to one another, and God was the source for it all.

"That's a great world," he said.

"It *was* a great world," she said.

GREEN

In de Lune, Caleb took another sip of his coffee and was surprised to find it still warm. The café's thick mugs retained the heat well. Overhead, U2's "Yahweh" played through the speakers. This was the perfect song for the moment, and he was glad to see Anna wanted to hear more.

"Before the world began, the Designer existed," Caleb said. "Like a loving artist, he created the world out of love, with love, to show love."

Anna rolled her eyes. "I've heard all this before," she said. Caleb knew she normally wouldn't tolerate religious talk like this and would end the discussion at this point. But this afternoon, she let him continue.

"I know. Hang on—there's more," he said. He remembered the first circle that the professor had drawn in her office. "In this perfect world all things were in right relationship with each other. At first, people and creation were on good footing."

His voice became stronger. "They took care of the planet instead of draining it of all of its oil and natural resources, instead of burning up rain forests for short-term crops, instead of creating artificial materials and polluting the rivers and oceans, instead of building dams to desecrate ecosystems, instead of releasing fluorocarbons into the air to deplete the ozone layer. People were called to take care of the planet, and that's what they did. We were supposed to manage it well, because it was not ours to own in the first place."

The bell jingled again and another small group of students walked into the café, but this time neither Anna nor Caleb noticed. Instead Anna smiled at Caleb, enjoying his passionate speech about the environment. She straightened up a little, leaned forward and rested her elbows on her knees, listening carefully.

WONDER

Caleb was no longer bothered by the loud conversation over in the other corner. He quit worrying about the loud music. He settled back into the cushioned couch.

"If being right with creation was the first thing, here's the second," Caleb continued. "People were right with each other. We didn't have to be selfish or look only to our own interests. We didn't ice people out of our relationships and make others feel inferior. We didn't blame others for our own wrongdoing. We didn't steal or oppress each other. All of the stuff in the news—none of it was in the original design. We weren't designed to gossip or hate based on skin color, nor were we made to kill entire groups of people out of revenge. We weren't meant to take advantage of the poor. We really loved each other. There was no shame in intimacy. We really wanted the best for each other, and enjoyed each other's company."

"What a wonderful world," Anna said, her flippant tone at odds with her flushed face and intense expression. Caleb wondered if she found the café stuffy too. Or maybe she was getting this in a new way. Or was her heart beating a little faster, the way Caleb's was? He soldiered on, determined not to get distracted.

"Sort of," he said. "But not wonderful in a dreamy way. It was real. It was what we've always longed for. You know how hard it is to be at home, right? Our parents never quite understood us. What if our families were actually meant to be places of love and support? What if we had friends who didn't hurt us but were always trustworthy? We all yearn for this deep down inside—we want to know and be known. And it was true once. It happened back then, and it was the world as it was intended to be."

"Go on," said Anna quietly, her eyes now slightly guarded.

"Our relationships with each other were great," he continued. "But so were our systems, and there wasn't anything in them that took advantage of weaker individuals. We took care of the planet, and it took care of us—mutual service. The systems were not designed to keep children in bonded labor in India or as sex slaves in Thailand. They weren't created so that a majority culture could oppress the minority, or so that corporations could rape underdeveloped countries of their resources and labor. No government was meant to blatantly deny human rights. No system was created for people to hurt each other—only to serve each other."

"Sure. But there were only two people back then, Cay," she said.

"Yeah, you got me," he said. "But the relationships between man, woman, the animals and all other parts of nature were all meant for love and service—not for taking advantage of each other. That's clear."

PROCESS

Anna was carefully processing everything she was hearing. She'd never known a Christian to talk about the environment before, let alone social justice issues. She'd thought most of them didn't care a fig's leaf about nature and its resources and were more interested in gadgets, movies and blogs. Instead of caring for the world around them, they preferred to huddle in their little cliques and sing cheesy songs.

But here was Caleb, discussing the same issues she cared about and worked tirelessly to bring awareness to on campus. And he was placing them in the context of religion.

When they'd first come to the café tonight she'd suspected—and half-hoped—that they might finally be having "the talk." But Caleb had a different talk in mind. Anna had thought it was just going to be more of the same, tired message she'd heard so many times before— and rejected. She normally didn't tolerate religious talk from anyone and cut off the discussion as soon as it began. But this was Caleb, so she let it continue.

No doubt, she liked to hear Caleb talk when he was passionate, even if it was about religion. And now he was saying that God had designed the planet to be free of oppression, free of sexism, racism and any other *-ism*.

"It's not the way the world is supposed to be," she'd said, and he had agreed. That comment, like breath, brought the message to life in a new way. And she'd felt something stirring in her chest—as quiet as a whisper—when he'd mentioned family. She needed to hear more.

"Okay, what's next?" she said.

INTIMACY

"Next, if people had a right relationship with the world, and right relationships with each other, they also had the most important right relationship of all—a relationship with God," started Caleb.

This was the point where Anna would normally break in and cut off
any further discussion. But she was invested at this point. So she remained silent, letting her friend continue.

"We didn't have an unhealthy fear of God," he said. "We weren't
worried that his followers would take advantage of us, using religion to
push their sociopolitical agendas on us. We didn't think about what God
might do if he or she really knew us. Back when all things were designed, our relationship with God was also one of intimacy, without fear
of shame. He loved us, and we loved him back. It's the most important
relationship of all . . ."

Caleb trailed off. He didn't want to sound too much like a televan-
gelist, so he summed it up. "All of creation was designed for good. God
himself called it 'very good.' It was made inherently good and made for
good purposes. What do you think?"

"It's not nearly as bad as I thought," Anna said. "And I like the en-
vironmental and justice stuff."

She took in another sip of her coffee and said, "So if we had such a wonderful world, then what happened? Why do we have the world today?"

Caleb smiled wide, raised his eyebrows and used his best cheesy voice. "I'm glad you asked."

Anna rolled her eyes.

PART TWO

Damaged by Evil

BISHOP

The late-lunch crowd ebbed away, and de Lune was emptier now. A small number of students kept on studying, leaving their empty coffee mugs out to guard their right to stay.

She's still listening, Caleb thought. His bar for the conversation wasn't high: if she didn't shut it down and forbid him to bring up Jesus ever again, he would consider that a success. Low expectations were sometimes useful. But she actually seemed interested in what he was saying.

"So the world and everything in it were designed for good," he said. "But people weren't satisfied, even in this good place. We didn't like taking orders, and we definitely didn't want someone else to have leadership over our lives, even if that someone else was far better qualified to run the place. Instead, we wanted to run this ship—this world—as captains. We wanted to be in charge, to take the Designer's place. We were going to live for ourselves and bend everything in creation to serve our own purposes and pleasures."

"But not everyone's like that," Anna said. "Are you saying all human beings are selfish?"

"Doesn't that make sense?" he replied. "Think about this: why do you do the things you do? Why do you go to school? Why are you taking your next job? Why do you wear the clothes you do? Why do you watch movies or buy CDs? Why did you choose your car? Or your friends? What would you say? Don't you just do these things for yourself?"

"Well—some things just are the way they are," she protested. "We need to go to school or get a job. It's one way we can help others. We need clothes on our backs. And I need to drive. Sure, we Americans spend far too much, but I try my best. And everyone needs friends. But I do want to help people along the way." She was getting annoyed again.

Caleb should have anticipated this. Anna *was* more thoughtful about her choices than most people, and she fought for causes that few else cared about. He knew she was being honest. She really did want to help people, particularly those who were powerless and defenseless.

Dumb, Caleb. He had donned his miter and aimed his accusing, gold-encrusted finger at her, scrutinizing her selfishness from his self-righteousness throne. But she wasn't any more selfish than many of the Christians he knew. Sure, people are selfish, but not *everything* people did was selfish, Christian or otherwise. So, the finger bent and pointed at his own heart. And the painted moon above kept on smiling.

PROPHET

"Sorry, Anna," he said. "My bad. I'm a dork. I like your answer better. Yeah, you want to help people along the way—and that's good. Sorry about that."

She appreciated the apology. "Sure, man. Just don't get on your high horse again, or I'll have to knock you off of it." She smiled and gave him a little shove with her forearm.

He laughed. "Okay, why do you think there's evil in the world?"

"That's a big question, Socrates. Well, I don't know about evil . . . but people definitely have incentives to oppress and hurt each other."

"What do you mean?" he asked. He was surprised at how quickly she'd come up with that answer.

"I'm talking about vicious cycles. They layer on top of each other until we jack everything up. It's crazy. Money is one layer: people hurt each other for more of it. They sell guns, drugs, sex or children for profit. They destroy lives while lining their pockets. It all sucks to hell. Even the government will bomb countries for their own oil interests, while corporations ruin the environment—because it's cheaper. Or did you hear about the twenty-five thousand Indian farmers who killed themselves in protest?"

Anna continued, building steam. "A decade ago, the World Bank forced India to open up its seed sector to 'help' with its economy. American corporations replaced the naturally reproducing cotton seed with patented, genetically sterilized seeds. Indian cotton farmers who would normally have saved some seed to plant the next crop couldn't do that anymore—they had to buy seeds and expensive pesticides from the corporations, which depleted their income and increased their debt. They couldn't even survive, so they started killing themselves in protest. That's oppression! Add corrupt governments and unjust laws, and it's easy to see that oppression and injustice happen everywhere. 'Injustice anywhere is a threat to justice everywhere.'"

Her voice was strong and intense, like the prophets of old. Caleb swore he heard the Holy Spirit speaking through her. If you plopped those words in the ocean, they would sink with truth and cause the waters to rise. Even if Caleb didn't agree with everything Anna said, there was a lot to learn about, grieve over and prayerfully act on. But he also squirmed when she talked about her politics—they were way further left than he was used to. He didn't want to become a liberal. Though that word meant two different things in religion and politics, it made conservatives in both camps equally nervous.

PLAIN

Anna shifted in her chair and continued her analysis. "Another layer is violence. Violence begets violence. Revenge gives birth to revenge. Air bombers produce suicide bombers. When you kill someone's mother or brother, they want to get back at you. Or at your country. Even religion gets into it: the Lord's Resistance Army in Uganda kidnaps children, brainwashes them and tells them God wants them to kill and rape others. That starts another cycle. It's all jacked up."

Caleb had an idea. "So why try and stop them?" he said calmly.

"What do you mean, Cay—they're just wrong." She squinted her eyes at him, clearly wondering if he was an idiot.

"But how can we say someone else is wrong?"

"Because it oppresses others—it's just *wrong!*" she said, her eyes alive with anger. Her fists clenched and unclenched.

"I hear you. But lots of people think we should let others do whatever they want. Can we really say people should do whatever they think is right? Can we really say someone should live by his or her standards and I'll live by mine? We can't, because one person's standards can hurt others—for example, one guy thinks sex trafficking is okay because it helps him make a lot of money, but it victimizes women. It's messed up. Yes, we need to be careful about judging others, but there are times when something is just plain *wrong*."

"Yeah, but that's different," Anna stared to say. Then she paused. She knew what Caleb was getting at, and she didn't like it. On one hand, she believed that some people had to change, to get involved with justice issues, even to change their buying habits. Yet they didn't, and it did upset her. A certain sweater could have been made in a sweatshop, funding the system that kept children in bonded slavery. If they bought an SUV, they were endangering the environment and other people on the road for their own comfort and safety. If they bought a certain diamond, they were supporting people who oppressed children in African mines to fund their civil wars.

But she also didn't want people telling her what to do with her life either. Especially when it came to religion. How did you know who was right and who was wrong? Yet she had to admit that some things were just plain wrong. Maybe other things could be just plain right.

SCREWED

"Maybe you've got a point there," she said with a scowl. "I know I don't want someone to mess with my life and tell me I'm wrong about something. But I guess that doesn't make sense. If I don't want anyone to tell me how to live my life, then I have no right to tell others how to live theirs—even those who are clearly doing wrong. That's inconsistent."

Caleb was shocked that she came to this conclusion on her own so quickly.

"Right," he said, "because some things really *are* wrong and evil. This may sound obvious, but many people do it because they don't love others. They make decisions based on their own desires and wants. Doesn't that make them gods, in a sense? And they're willing to make other people suffer for their own gain. That's injustice. That's evil."

Caleb looked down at his coffee swirling in his fidgeting hands. He kept his gaze there and said, "If I really look at my own life, I do the same things as well. Deep down, I don't love people like I could or should. It's way easy for me, in my everyday interactions, to stop loving people and try to use them for my own advantage, my own profit."

"C'mon, Cay. You're Mr. Goody-Two-Shoes." For once she wasn't being sarcastic.

"No, I'm not," he said slowly. "I think crappy things, even if I don't act on everything. A few days ago I was pissed off at my pastor. Again. I really thought I was right and that he was narrow-minded and didn't see the whole picture. He's a good guy—really he is—but he doesn't always get me. But by judging him, I oppress him too. We all have power to oppress others in some way, and I oppressed him in my mind. Because I didn't really love him—at least, not at that moment. Sure, I didn't use a fist or gun—sticks and stones may break our bones but words can wound a soul. I'm no better than anyone else."

"Then we're all screwed. Everyone does that."

"And that's precisely the problem. Even if I stop doing wrong things, I don't love people around me the way I should. You're right: we're all screwed. That's how we get a world like this. Look around. Evil. Everywhere. All around us and all in us. We've been left unchecked and need some resources to help fight against the system, against others who are oppressing. We even fight ourselves: we don't often do what we know we should."

"So you're saying that I might also be a part of the problem and might not even know it?" She stared out the window, following a few passers-by with her eyes.

ENGINE

Shalandra and Caleb each sat in front of a steaming slice of pepperoni and mushroom pizza, a side salad and a soft drink. She had sprinkled a few flakes of chili pepper on her slice.

It was their third meeting, almost a year ago. Shalandra had left her lunch at home, which was a great excuse to get a couple of slices. Since the sun was peeking out from behind the clouds, they'd felt invited to take a stroll to Giuseppe's on the Ave. Seattleites had to take advantage of the sun whenever it appeared.

Giuseppe's was a basic pizza parlor with Italian movie posters on the brick walls and green, red and white accents everywhere. But they weren't here for the décor: Giuseppe's made one of the best New York style pizzas in town—the kind you could fold up and gobble down as a makeshift calzone. Even at this hour, the plastic booths were full. Shalandra joked that Giuseppe's must put crack in the sauce—one bite left you irrationally wanting more.

Their Bibles and her notepad had already found their places on the table. Shalandra drew a second circle next to the first one on the same diagram she had started in their previous meeting. This circle was jagged on the outside with some stick figures in the center of it:

"Before we start, there's something we need to go over," she said. "First, God designed the world. So he knows better than anyone what it's supposed to do. Imagine that I designed the latest car engine for Honda. I know, huge stretch. I wish I did know something about cars, because I just had to pay seven hundred dollars to replace my brakes and rotors."

Caleb listened politely, but she cut herself off, laughing and gently slapping the table. "I sound bitter, don't I? Anyway, if I were the car engine's designer, then I would know best what each part of the engine was supposed to do, how it was supposed to interact with other parts, what to put into the engine for maximum performance and what the potential breakdowns might be. I would know best how to maintain it and keep it running." Caleb nodded.

"Good. So, in the same way, if God designed the world and everything in it, he would know best what each part was supposed to do, how it was supposed to interact with other parts, and what it would take to maintain this beautiful new world. But what if God gave the main part of the engine a mind of its own? What if a part—like a spark plug or something—was allowed to choose whether to fire or not, regardless of whatever happened in the engine's system? The hope would be that the spark plug would fire correctly on its own accord, but the possibility existed for it to fire in a way that could ruin the engine."

"Free will," he said.

"Yes. With free will, God endows us with great power—to choose good and be a blessing, or to choose evil and be a curse. Our actions affect others. So God sets out some guidelines for the good functioning of the planet, but people have the freedom to choose it or not." She took another bite of her pizza.

"But why would God take such a risk? I mean, wouldn't it be better if he forced us to do the right thing all the time? Then we wouldn't have the problems we have today, right?"

"Maybe. But God loves us too much to control us like that. Let's see . . . have you ever been in love?"

Caleb sat paralyzed, not knowing how to answer. He had definitely liked the girl he'd dated in high school, but did that count as love? What was Shalandra's definition of love?

"When you're in love, you want what's best for the other person," she said, letting him off the hook. "You bend over backward to help them, even if at times it hurts you. And all you want in return is their love. But you can't force it. You love that person too much to coerce them to love you back. So you hope or wait or trust. But you do not force. God is the same way. He won't ever force us to do something, but he'll try to win us over and hope that we love him back. He won't step on our free will or he would be more manipulative and less loving."

"But what about predestination? Isn't God in control? How can he be in control if—"

"That's a huge question," she said, dropping her slice to show him how large with her hands outstretched. "Let's bring up that question later if you need to, but first we need to finish the framework."

Caleb's brow scrunched up and he stared down at his empty paper plate. He wouldn't be able to move on without addressing this issue, even though he knew scholars had debated it for centuries.

"Okay," sighed the professor in resignation. "Take this for now, and we'll probably have to come back to it later. God's clearly in control. That's in the Bible. But we also have free will. That's in the Bible too. So I think that God is fully in control yet we fully have free will. I'm not sure how that all pans out, but if Jesus can be fully human and fully divine and we're able to live with that paradox, then our entering into an eternal kind of life is fully God's choosing and yet fully our choosing. Is that all right for now?"

That was a bit mushy, Caleb thought. But he could live with it for the moment. It captured the mystery of the issue better than anything else he'd heard so far, so he made a quick mental note—*ask about predestination later*—and gave the professor his full attention.

RUIN

Shalandra took a sip of her soda while Caleb wondered if he should buy another slice of pizza. His first had gone down quickly, but he didn't want to interrupt. He took a long pull on his own soda instead.

"So in our free will," she continued, "we could choose to follow God or our own impulses. In the early Genesis account, human beings chose the latter. In Genesis 3, the serpent deceives Eve, encouraging her to question God's design for the place. He ultimately makes his final challenge. Check out Genesis 3:4-5."

Caleb read the passage aloud: "'You will not certainly die,' the serpent said to the woman. 'For God knows that when you eat of it your eyes will be opened, and you will be like God, knowing good and evil.'" He paused. "I've always had a question about this. Why does God want to keep them from knowing good and evil? Wouldn't he want them to know the difference?" He'd asked this question before but had never gotten a good answer.

"Good question. God always intended us to know the difference between good and evil. He'd already given us one command: do not eat from this particular tree. People began to know what was good—in step with God's design—and what was not good—out of step with

God's design. And good was what was good for the planet, remember? The Designer knew what was needed for creation to run well. But people didn't care about God's design anymore. They wanted to make their own designs. That's the great temptation: people want to be their own gods and create their own values. That way there's no one else to worship, no one to keep us accountable for doing right. We become the sole, unchallenged leaders of our lives and the planet. We do what we want, and usually that means doing things without regard to other people. Thus we damage ourselves and others because of our own selfishness."

She noticed that a few drops of pizza sauce had splattered on the notepad. She rubbed them out as best as she could with a napkin, then drew four arrows that pointed inward with accusation:

Makes sense, he thought. Life wasn't just about falling in line with the Bible—it was more than that. Since God had designed the world so that everything in it could bless and serve everything else, following our own selfish designs gummed up the works and stalled the engine. Rejecting God's design wasn't just rejecting a religion but rejecting the way the world truly was and choosing to mess it up for our own gain and fame. For the first time in a while, faith felt like it had some footing in reality.

"That's what the Bible calls sin, right?" Caleb said.

"Yes. But it's not like a D-minus on your report card. It's not just saying something stupid to your teacher in class." Here she gave him a wink. "It's not just the accumulation of sins, but *sin*. A sinful nature— like damage or disease, a general leaning in our spirit that makes it easier for us to damage all things in the planet, our relationships and our own center of being: our souls."

EPIDEMIC

A group of students walked by, pizzas in hand, and sat at the booth behind the professor. The aroma of tomato, garlic, basil and mozzarella wafted over to Caleb, enticing him again to consider another slice. He felt the pizza withdrawal pangs in his stomach. Yet still he resisted.

"It's going to get ugly," Shalandra said, "because the world goes from bad to worse. In Genesis 3, Adam and Eve chose against the Designer. As a result they felt shame. Weird. Nothing changed on the outside—they were still naked as always. But now they knew they were naked. So they tried to cover themselves with leaves. They must have felt downright awful, because that couldn't have been easy. Adam blamed Eve, and then he had the guts to blame God for making her in the first place: 'The woman you put here with me . . .' Eve also attempted to shift the blame and say it wasn't her fault. We now have cycles of shame and blame."

She drew a squiggly line in her diagram, like a curtain that kept the stick figures apart:

Designed for good

"It got worse," she continued. "In Genesis 4, Cain killed Abel out of envy—Abel's offering was accepted by God while Cain's was not. So he committed the first murder in history, destroying someone else's happiness so he could feel better about himself. But it still got worse. Read Genesis 4:23-24 for me." She took another sip of her soda, as Caleb read.

"Lamech said to his wives, 'Adah and Zillah, listen to me; wives of Lamech, hear my words. I have killed a man for wounding me, a young man for injuring me. If Cain is avenged seven times, then Lamech seventy-seven times.'"

"Lamech took murder to a new level," the professor said. "He killed people just for wounding him. He was willing to deal revenge and escalate violence up to seventy-seven times. Then it got even worse. He married two women—the first instance of polygamy—and check out the meaning of their names: Adah means 'ornament' and Zillah means 'shadow.' Women went from saving with strength to being ornaments and shadows. Sad, huh? Polygamy was never meant to happen. God did not create Adam and Eve and Jen and Tonya. Through these women's names, the biblical author makes it clear that all further mistreatment of women was because of our rebellion against the Designer's plans."

Caleb leaned back so quickly that he bumped heads with a woman sitting behind him. He quickly apologized and rubbed the back of his head. He had never heard a cogent argument against polygamy from the Bible before. It seemed that Old Testament figures often had many wives, and he had wondered what the biblical standard for polygamy really was. But he now saw that God loved them despite his disapproval in this area.

"But it got still worse," she said. "Read Genesis 6:2."

"The sons of God saw that these daughters were beautiful, and they married any of them they chose."

"What's your translation?" she asked, and Caleb showed her. "Interesting. You have *married* in your version, but the Hebrew word is *took*. Now look at Genesis 4:1. I think your version says Adam 'made love' with Eve, but the Hebrew is *knew*. 'To know' was their slang for sex. It's a great word about intimacy, being close with someone else instead of using them. In a way, sex *is* knowing someone. That's what happened with Adam and Eve. But by chapter 6, the self-proclaimed sons of God were taking instead of knowing. They could have been doing something benign, but more likely they were forcing marriages or, at the worst, raping women. At any rate, women who once saved with strength were now objects like ornaments and shadows to be taken by men."

Taking instead of knowing—wasn't that what lust was? Caleb saw how everything was connected. The Genesis account described an ugly whirlpool of sin and oppression against women that kept on sucking light, life and all of creation down into its vortex. Anna needed to hear this.

"It went from bad to worse," Shalandra said ominously. "Read Genesis 6:5-6."

"The Lord saw how great the wickedness of the human race had become on the earth, and that every inclination of the thoughts of the human heart was only evil all the time. The Lord regretted that he had made human beings on the earth, and his heart was deeply troubled."

"God was grieved, and he regretted making the world," the profes-sor said. "'His heart was full of pain.' It's one of the saddest notes in the Bible. The world was going downhill. God was sorry he made people, and people were afraid of God. Our relationship with God was in com-plete disarray, and the world and everything in it was damaged by evil."

Shalandra drew another inner circle, marring it with another squiggly line. She wrote the words "Damaged by evil" on top of the new circle:

Caleb had never seen these themes played out so clearly in the early chapters of the Bible, especially the theme of sin against women. "It's not the way it's supposed to be." Where God had wanted his image bearers to multiply and fill the earth, people had multiplied and filled the earth with something that reeked to heaven, something unholy and evil. If he ever had the chance, Caleb was going to share all of this with Anna.

RAIN

Shalandra looked at her watch. "Let's head back. But we'll keep on talking along the way."

They bussed their table, crossed the street and walked south back toward her office. The sun had hidden behind the clouds again and it was starting to drizzle. Of course they didn't have umbrellas. Caleb's fingers suddenly felt cold, and he blew on them to warm them up. He shivered and felt his stomach stir. *I hope I'm not getting sick,* he thought. Still, he and Shalandra strode down the Ave at a brisk pace.

The professor picked up the conversation right where they'd left it. "So as we've seen, the planet has hit a low point and God is sorry he made it. As we move on in Genesis, he decides to start over. He brings rain—the first time water falls from the sky in the Bible—and every living creature is destroyed. But God saves Noah and his family on the ark. Now get this: How do you think Noah feels when the rains come *again?*"

She held out her hand, catching some droplets. "Probably scared out of his mind, right? But God has created the rainbow as a sign of his promise never to destroy the earth with water again. Do you see the redemption here? It's precisely in the rains that God gives his sign—a mix of glorious light and dreaded water. Noah doesn't have to fear the rain again. In the Genesis story, it's a brief glimmer of hope before things go bad again."

Caleb held out his hands to feel the rain as well. He understood the power of this story: God could take his greatest pain and through it bring a great promise. God did it with Jesus, taking his greatest pain for the greatest healing on the planet. Whatever fear he might feel, he could walk in faith knowing that rainbows only appear in the rain.

COLOR

Caleb smiled as they walked, appreciating the Genesis walk-through. He knew it was important. *In the beginning.* Whenever he'd sat through biology class he'd felt that the Bible had to be put on hold. But now he saw how Genesis shaped the beginnings of a Christian worldview and explained human interactions in a way that felt real.

Shalandra continued. "In Genesis 11—without getting into the whole story—race, ethnicity and culture become issues that separate people from one another, and the world is damaged in a new way: black against white, Korean against Japanese, Indian against Pakistani, Arab against Jew."

Caleb turned toward her as if he'd been pulled up hard by a set of reins. "Can we talk about that a bit, professor? It seems that ethnicity is a curse in the tower of Babel account, doesn't it? Shouldn't we just be colorblind? Then wouldn't we all just get along?"

Shalandra paused in thought, though her feet kept moving. She looked at him with a furrowed brow.

"That's Interesting," she said. "You called it a 'curse.' But that word doesn't show up in the passage. God confuses their language because they're settling down by building a city instead of doing what he'd asked in Genesis 1:28—to multiply and fill the earth. It wasn't a curse. It was helping them along in their calling."

I need to check that, Caleb thought.

"We're not called to be colorblind at all," she continued. "In creation, God made a variety of animals and plant life, right? And in Genesis 10, before Babel, there's a list of people of different languages, cultures and backgrounds that theologians call the 'table of nations.' In Acts 2, people in the crowd at Pentecost hear Peter's message in their own language, not in Aramaic. See, the Spirit honors culture and language instead of ignoring it. More importantly, Revelation 7:9 says that people of every nation, tribe and language will worship God at the end of time. The word 'nation' is *ethnos* in Greek, where we get the word 'ethnicity.'"

Shalandra kept going—she was on a roll. "At the end of history, we'll keep our ethnicity and culture. We won't lose it; it will be redeemed. We'll no longer fight each other but be reconciled. We'll speak different languages but understand each other perfectly. We're not to be colorblind but color-embracing. If it's in God's kingdom at the end, can ethnicity and culture be a curse? It can't be. It must be good and intended."

Culture and ethnicity at the end of time? Caleb hadn't thought about that before. He'd honestly thought that heaven would be a giant melting pot where ethnicity didn't exist. But if he started to picture heaven in his mind, he saw white robes. And mostly white people. At least, everyone spoke English. But now . . . would he be Korean in heaven?

This line of thinking brought up another question: "But doesn't the Bible say that there is now neither male nor female, Jew nor Greek, slave nor free because we're all one in Christ Jesus?" Caleb asked.

The professor made a gesture of impatience. It was apparent that she'd heard this question a few times before. She stopped walking and turned to Caleb. "Is it okay to be a man of God or a woman of God? Do you approve of men's studies and women's studies—I mean, in the church, is it okay to have men's groups and women's groups?"

"Yeah, of course," he said.

"Don't you see the parallel?" she asked. "We use that verse to say that race, ethnicity and culture don't matter—only that we're Christians. And in our society we think our ethnic identity markers are wrong and that we should stop being so black or so Mexican and just be American, right?"

Caleb didn't say anything. He'd had that exact thought in his ethnic studies classes, believing it to be essentially biblical, but he'd had enough savvy not to say anything. There was no way he wanted to be fed to the secular lions of the university's coliseum. But now it was his mentor questioning him. He felt like he was being led to the burning stake and hoped that this would all end well.

"Sorry, Caleb," Shalandra said, noticing his defensive posture. "I get a little carried away sometimes."

Caleb relaxed his shoulders and chuckled. "No problem. But you're right; I was getting a little nervous."

"I understand," she said. "But do you see how our interactions over race and ethnicity contribute in their own way to the damage?"

He nodded. Yeah, it was always tough to talk about racial issues.

"Okay, let's back up," she said. "We allow a person to be a man or a woman of God, right? Why not allow someone to be an Indian of God or a Kenyan of God or a multiracial person of God or even a third-culture person of God? It does get complex, I know. But consider this: we know the ethnicity of every character who has a name in the Bible—not one is lost on us. We know about Uriah the Hittite and Cornelius the Italian. In America, on the other hand, race is taboo. We can't talk about it without someone getting upset. Our history and its racial ten-

sions, which have created some of the largest clashes of our time, make
us hesitant to acknowledge race. But our ethnic identity is part of our
journey in faith, and unless we learn how to embrace the way God has
made us—ethnicity and all—then we won't ever realize our full potential as ministers of reconciliation."

"But how?" Caleb protested. "I don't understand how it will help
us become better reconcilers. Don't we get along better if we stop di-
viding ourselves along ethnic lines?"

"That verse you quoted is not about getting rid of gender, race or
class markers," Shalandra said. "You would be offended if someone
told you, 'I don't really consider you a man of God,' right? Aren't you
a man? You accept that marker easily. Why not enjoy your ethnic identity as well? Racial tensions won't go away if we ignore them. We have
to face them, own our ethnicities and receive their blessing, and then
we turn around and be a blessing to others. I was at a Christian conference once where Japanese delegates tearfully asked for forgiveness
from the Koreans, and vice versa. You couldn't have scripted that kind
of thing. Forgiveness wasn't exchanged by individuals but by entire ethnic groups and nations. I couldn't help but think that this was a taste
of heaven. And there are more stories like that one throughout the
world. But for many, race and ethnicity still divide us, and ignoring
them won't help us address the damage to our world."

Caleb's grandparents had talked about their experiences under Japanese occupation, so he knew full well the tension that existed between
Japanese and Korean people. His grandparents still didn't buy anything
Japanese-made. Clearly these issues were continuing to tear people
apart.

BLING

They started walking again and took a left on Campus Parkway to head back toward the main part of campus.

Shalandra went on. "Slave or free. Not only do American Christians need to embrace their ethnicity, but also their class identity as well. We're rich, but we think we're poor because materialism runs rampant here. And I'm a part of it. It's not easy fighting the urge to buy something just because I can. It's an epidemic, spreading through music, movies, TV, cultural expectations, friends, family members. It's very hard to escape. It's frankly scary how easy it is to worship wealth and then ask God to bless it. But Jesus is clear that we cannot worship both God and money. If we owned the fact that all of us Americans are richer than most everyone else on the planet, then perhaps we would be moved to give more away. It's easier to think we're poor—or just 'middle class'—because it costs us less. But it's just not true for most of us."

That's true, Caleb thought. The lure of materialism was easy to recognize yet tough to deal with in his own life.

She kept going. "I recently read that, in 2000, only the gross domestic product of Japan and the United States beat the income of American evangelicals. Only two countries. One-fifth of what American evangeli-

cals make in a year would erase the world debt of the sixty poorest nations. That floored me, and I started to spend less and give more away.
It's sad when we think we're poor because we can't afford a 3,000-
square-foot house near Lake Washington when the world's poor live in
shantytowns throughout the planet. And we could do so much if we just
owned our class identity and received its blessings and let Jesus use it
for the good of others, instead of just feeling guilty about it or wishing
we had more. If we remembered that we're rich, we might stop accu-
mulating oversized homes or luxury cars or just *more* of anything and
give more away. Our world is certainly damaged by our constant need
for more."

Caleb didn't mean to be confrontational, but he wanted more answers. "All right, so what about you?" he asked. "It seems like you
have a great job and a beautiful office. You admit that you live in a nice
part of town. You probably have a nice ride. What do you do?"

"That's fair," she replied. "And that's exactly what I'm saying. I'm
not poor. I'm not trying to glamorize poverty. I'm trying to own the fact
that compared to the rest of the world, I *am* rich. I'm definitely not the
richest in this town, but I know I have a lot of stuff. There's nothing
wrong with being rich, as long as I understand that my wealth is not for
me. It's meant to bless others. So I make an extra effort to give more
away. I've learned to live on half of my take-home pay. I save some and
give about a third away to charities I trust or people who need it. And
I'm telling you, Jesus cares how I spend my money. Did you know that
he talked about money more than any other topic except the kingdom
of God? One out of every nine verses in Luke is about money. So I'm
trying my best to pay attention."

Caleb remembered Manila and his friends who lived in the slum.
What they'd taught him was far more tangible and intuitive than what
he could learn from any theoretical discussion. Even as a college stu-

dent he had much more than they did. His own materialism—perhaps a whole nation's—was tied into the system of planetwide damage.

Suddenly the blood drained from his face and he started to feel weak. His stomach turned. The rain's chill didn't help. He grabbed the rail near the bottom of the overpass to steady himself. Then he looked up at Shalandra.

"Caleb," she asked, "Are you okay?"

He shook his head and clutched his stomach with his free hand. "Excuse me—" he said, then bolted toward the nearest bathroom.

FINGER

The couches at de Lune had a magical quality about them. No matter how long you sat in them, they always felt comfortable. Whether you leaned back, sat up or shifted around, the velvet couches felt like clouds, except you didn't fall through.

Anna was still staring out of the window. Her thoughts turned to her family, and she drifted back to her last shouting match with her father.

But Caleb was recalling the second circle of the professor's diagram. "So when we look at our planet, the stuff you fight all the time— racism, materialism, human trafficking, pollution, poverty—they're created not merely by 'systems' out there; they're generated by us and through us. Our culture is full of systems: governments, corporations, media and culture, and we're all a part of them. These systems affect us, influence us and cause us to make decisions—for good or for bad. As you've said, these systems are damaged and often hurt us. And we contribute to the damage. Know what I mean?"

"Definitely," she said, jolted back to the present. She liked hearing a Christian talk about the major issues on the planet. Christians could be so myopic.

"Then there are problems on a relational level. Someone hurts us, either knowingly or unknowingly, and we hurt them back. We're in a world of walking wounded, all jabbing each other with insults, comparisons, expectations. It happens all the time and we no longer function out of our purpose: for love."

"Ah, for love," she said, clasping her hands together. She loved teasing him about his idealism, though she suffered the same dreams. She was just better at hiding some of it.

"Well—yeah," he said, a little put off, "but not in that way. We really don't even know how to love. We're damaged. Sometimes we escape into our addictions, like pornography or shopping. We numb ourselves from the reality that life is full of suffering. We can't take this world as it is. Or we cope by building empires so we don't have to deal with the world on its terms but on our own terms instead. We try to have enough power, whether through wealth, status or popularity, that we can shelter ourselves from everything out there. But they trap us and make us prisoner."

He pointed at himself for emphasis. "We wanted to be captains but we found ourselves chained to the oars, the oars of what we need to have or be. We're not captains but slaves. And we've steered ourselves away from love and toward evil. I know that sounds harsh, but what's easier to do: the right thing or the wrong thing? It doesn't even matter how you gauge right or wrong—what's easier to do?"

She thought for a moment. "Definitely the wrong thing," she said. "Skip class or do homework. Ignore pain or do justice. Keep someone at a distance or forgive them."

"Yeah," said Caleb. "We have a disease that makes it easier to do what's wrong than what's right or loving. Without any moral guidance, we flounder, creating a world that's going from bad to worse. We're not what we were designed to be. We're nothing close. We need a cure to help us become the people we truly want to be. Because in our sickness

we've hurt our planet, our friends, our family, our neighbors and ourselves along the way. This is not the way it's supposed to be. It's not the
way it was designed. We're defacing the work of art that God made
called creation."

It was starting to sound preachy to Anna, but the evidence of a
planet gone awry was overwhelming. She knew that the great blue orb
she lived on was truly infected with some sort of disease. And if there
was a cure, she wanted to know about it.

"So we're basically giving the Designer the big middle finger, right?"
She grinned and flipped Caleb off.

Anna felt like Caleb had pulled back the curtains and helped her see the entire stage. His message seemed larger in scope than anything she'd heard in church before. Christians never seemed to care about anything more than church attendance and Bible reading. Or abortion and homosexuality. But Caleb was talking about something much larger. She had always thought her political leanings and passions were alien to the church. Now she wondered if she might have a place in the faith after all. Maybe.

But, she was beginning to feel cooped up in the café. "You wanna head back?" she asked. "We can talk along the way."

Caleb downed the last gulp of his now-cold coffee, and they started walking south on the Ave. As they left the café, he noticed a group of students walking toward them, all stylishly dressed, some of them with cigarettes in their hands. They spoke Korean to each other and didn't smile much.

Caleb recognized a few of his friends and called out, "Hey, guys! What's up? Where are you going?"

They stopped, and John, who seemed to be the leader, said, "Making a *boba* run, man. *Gah-leh?*"

"Sounds good," said Caleb. He liked bubble tea. "But I can't. Let me know the next time you're heading out, though."

"Cool, man. Later," and the group went on their way before Caleb could introduce Anna. As they waved goodbye, two girls in the group passed over Anna with their eyes, like an airport security check.

"Who are they?" asked Anna.

"Some KSA friends of mine."

"*Friendly,* aren't they?"

"Yeah," he smiled. "Don't be too hard on them. They're a good crew. It just takes them a while to warm up."

Anna hadn't pegged Caleb for a KSA type, but he wouldn't have pegged himself as one either. The fact that Caleb had friends in the Korean Students Association was evidence that God had been changing his heart over the past year.

MAN

The evening after Giuseppe's hadn't been easy. He'd made frequent trips to the toilet, trying to get over a bout of food poisoning. Maybe Shalandra was right: maybe they did put crack in the sauce. At the same time he was still trying to digest what she'd said to him during their discussion

He had an easier time with her version of the predestination–free will debate. In the past he would have thought her explanation a cop-out. But now he believed it was biblical, even though messy and myste-rious. His more theologically astute buddies would probably snub their noses at him, but if that was the worst of it, he could handle it.

What she'd said about ethnic identity, on the other hand, shook his mind like an Etch-A-Sketch, leaving him with a blank slate. He queried Tom about it the next day.

"Hey, are you a man of God?" he asked. Caleb and Tom were study-ing in the library as usual, along with Dave. Of the three, Dave looked the oldest: he was tall, lean and had a goatee. And he seemed uncom-fortably cramped at his carrel. But Tom was the loudest, and his round belly shook whenever he laughed, which was often.

"Uh, seriously?" Tom said, looking up from his book with eyebrows raised. "Sure, why do you ask?"

"Okay, then, are you a Mexican man of God?" Caleb asked, even though technically only Tom's mother was Mexican.

"Dude, what's up with you?"

After explaining what he'd discussed with Shalandra, Tom responded, "Well then, according to Professor Jones, I guess I am. Or at least half." He laughed, and his shoulders shook.

Tom turned to Dave and said in a loud voice, "Hey, Dave. Are you a white man of—"

"Shut up, man!" Caleb hissed. Tom smiled mischievously. Caleb turned to Dave and said, "It's nothing." Dave just shrugged and went back to studying.

WATER

A few days later Caleb had taken a walk on campus in the late afternoon to mull over what Shalandra had said. The day had been relatively clear, so he'd started walking toward Drumheller Fountain. In front of him the Suzallo Library and Gerberding building perfectly framed a stunning panorama with snow-capped Mt. Rainier as its centerpiece. By design the architects had rotated the orientation of the lower campus to preserve this view. Its beauty reminded him how gifted the Designer truly was.

He had always hung on to Paul's words in Galatians: "There is neither Jew nor Gentile, slave nor free, neither male nor female for all are one in Christ Jesus." He'd thought that this verse compelled him to ignore racial markers. But he was starting to see it as a statement of value—all are one because our primary identity is in Jesus. The professor was right: it didn't necessarily mean we should get rid of the identity markers. He was, after all, a man of God, right?

Caleb could see that this concept wasn't a big deal to Tom. Why was it a big deal to him? Maybe because he was using theology as an excuse to ignore his own personal issues. Theology as escape? That scared him a little. Wasn't theology supposed to be the timeless truth of God?

He knew he'd chosen to go to Experience in large part to escape the Asian bubble. Sure, he told himself and others that he was connecting with different kinds of people. But whenever he saw a group of Asians, he felt an adverse gut reaction. He didn't want to be seen with them. If he was honest, he didn't even like them. He wished they wouldn't just hang out by themselves in their cliques. He wished they wouldn't speak just their own languages. Whenever Asians around him were too "Asian"—he didn't even know what he meant by that— it made him uneasy.

I never think that about my white friends, he realized. When the Lambda Mus on Greek Row hung out together, he didn't think twice about it. He never once questioned the cliquishness of white people. Or African Americans for that matter. Or MEChA, the Latino group. He had been harder on Asians than anyone else.

He started to circle Drumheller Fountain and wondered why he was so uncomfortable around Koreans. The words from a sermon Pastor Jeff had once given popped into his head: *What we're annoyed by in others is what we hate most about ourselves.* He finally had words for it: *I'm ashamed of being Korean.*

It was easy to embrace one side of his hyphenated identity. He was born in Seattle and considered himself an American. If he wanted to he could run for president. But the Korean side represented all that was abominable. Sure, he loved the food. But he hated the Korean church and the hypocrisy and the materialism of the older generation. He abhorred being forced to obey his elders even if they were wrong. And were they stubborn. And difficult. He didn't want to have anything to do with them.

But there was a great cultural and church heritage to embrace: the food—ah, the *galbi*—the polyrhythmic music, the passion, the tireless praying, the community, the willingness to suffer. There were good things that were hard to see. According to Shalandra, God had designed him that way—Korean and American—not by accident but by design. He needed to embrace that, didn't he?

He stopped in his tracks and turned toward Mt. Rainier. He stepped toward the fountain's edge and turned his eyes toward the giant hill. His throat tightened.

"Forgive me, Father," he whispered. "I haven't trusted you. I thought you made a mistake, making me Korean. Help me embrace who you've made me to be. Help me, Father, to embrace being Korean American. I am a Korean American man of God, as you designed me to be."

He stretched out his arms, closed his eyes and kept on praying. The fountain's spray formed cloudlets that sprinkled on him, washing over him. He let the waters do to him what they'd done to millions over the centuries. The old passed away, the new came. In that moment thanksgiving was resurrected. Freedom loosened his face and he smiled wider than he had in a long time. Then he turned to walk back to his car.

The next day when he saw people from the Korean Students Association near Odie, he didn't recoil. He didn't breathe in cigarette smoke but true breath, wind and spirit. He looked over and smiled. Then he walked up and introduced himself. He realized that Jesus was with him, helping him love—even himself.

PART THREE

Restored for Better

HISTORY

"At least they could've introduced themselves," Anna said.

"That's true," said Caleb, but he was already thinking about getting back to the conversation they'd been having at de Lune. Setting up the problem of sin wasn't too hard—there was so much evidence all around. But he feared that the solution might sound too "Christianese" to her. Looking back, he didn't even know if he'd had the answers a year ago. But he was more sure nowadays—or at least more trusting—that he actually had good news to share. He hoped Anna wouldn't check out once they started talking about Jesus, about his life and message. She'd said Jesus was cool, right?

They crossed Fifteenth Avenue and turned right into the main entrance of the University of Washington. The street, Memorial Way, was lined on both sides by more than a hundred sycamores standing at attention—the original fifty-seven had been planted to honor the UW faculty and students killed in World War I. The Seattle winter had shaken off the trees' broad green leaves so they stood tall and naked. Perhaps they, like Adam and Eve, felt shame.

"So," as he picked up their conversation from the café, "do we agree that our world is damaged?"

"Sure," she said as they headed into the oldest part of the campus. On their right, they passed the oldest university museum on the West Coast, apparently old enough to capture the only dinosaur skeletons in the Northwest, including a stegosaurus. On their left was an observatory, another of UW's oldest buildings. It looked out at stars, nebulas and galaxies even more ancient than theirs. From this place, history almost seemed to call out to them.

"But God loved the world too much to let it stay that way. If someone was beating up your little sister, it wouldn't be loving to stand by and watch. You'd do something about it. So over two thousand years ago, God saw the evil on the planet and his heart broke, so he decided to do something about it. He came to the planet as a baby . . ."

"Christmas," she said, half-dancing as if she were partying on a late-night cable channel. "Consumerism . . . gone . . . wild!"

"For sure," he said, laughing. "Now, imagine if Bono came over to your house. Wouldn't you be a little awed? Imagine someone even more powerful, someone who literally used to come in clouds and thunder. Did you know that the word *voice* in Hebrew is the same for thunder? So when the Israelites heard God's voice, they heard his rumble and crackle. He would've been deathly intimidating. But God wanted to be with us and love us. So he came as the most helpless and dependent being in the universe: a baby. Sure, he might have been cute. But he was also diapers, spit-up and tears. He was human, with humanity's mess and insecurity, so that we could connect with him."

"Waxing poetic, aren't we?" Anna said. The sweet baby Jesus of Hallmark fame seemed sanitized to her, like a fairy tale. Everyone looked so peaceful in the pictures. And plastic. They didn't even need candles: Mary, Joseph and Jesus all had glowing heads to light up the stable, as if they'd drunk radioactive Kool-Aid. Sweet baby Jesus felt like fantasy, but she could relate to a messy, human Jesus.

"Jesus grew up in a town called Nazareth," Caleb continued, "learning the family trade as a building contractor. But when he turned thirty, he started to teach people the way we all should live. And it was radical: feed the hungry, clothe the naked, visit the prisoner, care for the widow, forgive those who hurt us. He was reminding the people of God how they should be acting, showing us a way to resist evil without defeated resignation or violent uprising. He taught us how to be transformed and then transform the planet. He ushered in something new— a God-empowered resistance movement against all that is evil in us and around us. He called that something the kingdom of God."

As Anna listened to Caleb, she thought for a moment that Jesus would be someone worth learning from. But she locked onto that last phrase: "Kingdom of God? Ah, I remember this stuff. Heaven, right? The afterlife with angels and everything?"

"Yup. Heaven," he said. "But it's not quite what you think."

TRUMPET

A year ago, Caleb had had to get to the other side of campus through a downpour. He'd been on his way to meet the professor for the fourth week in a row. He had recovered from the food poisoning and was feeling much better since the last time they'd seen each other.

Like a running back he jogged through campus, using the buildings as blockers from the soaking blitz. He finally made it to Padelford Hall, where Shalandra's office was located, and after he wiped his shoes on the industrial black doormat, he waited impatiently for the slow elevator. In her office finally, he sat down in the now-familiar chair that hugged and held him up.

Shalandra welcomed him with a cup of peppermint tea, still steaming in the white-and-purple UW mug. The mug's printed mascot—a husky—smiled at him, ready to bound out and merrily lick his face. She cupped her hands around her own mug of chamomile and brought it close to her face, allowing the vapors to waft up her nose and throat and cloud her glasses.

"I've got a cold," she said. She sounded like a muted trumpet.

"Why don't you go home?" Caleb started, but she just shook her head. So he gave up. "Well, I hope you feel better soon."

"Thanks. Are you feeling better, Caleb?"

"Yeah, it must've been something I ate. I'm fine and ready to go." He gave her a thumbs-up.

"Good to hear. But I'm sorry again about last time, Caleb. I got impatient with you. It's not an excuse, but I was tired and in a hurry to get back to the office. I've heard those questions many times before, and sometimes it feels like I have to repeat myself over and over again—" She covered her mouth and coughed hard.

"No problem, professor," he said, still a little worried for her. "I'm really thankful for what you said." He told her about his experience at Drumheller Fountain.

Shalandra beamed at him through puffy eyes. "That's great! I couldn't be happier for you." She blew over the top of the tea to cool it down and took a sip. "Okay, ready for the next part?"

Caleb nodded. He hadn't thought about it before, but sitting in a comfortable chair, holding a warm beverage in your hands and having a great conversation while it rained outside would be a great way to spend eternity. In this office, it was as if the drizzle provided the pitter-patter melodies to pacify his soul.

The professor pulled out her notepad and drew a new, jagged circle in the bottom right-hand corner and an arrow from above pointing directly to a cross in the center:

Designed for good

Damaged by evil

"Caleb," she said, "you already know about how God came to the planet as Jesus two thousand years ago. I like the way *The Message* puts it: he 'moved into the neighborhood.' Jesus became one of us to teach us—to show us in word and deed how to truly live."

"Gotcha," he said. This wasn't new to him. He sipped hesitantly on his tea, not wanting to burn his tongue.

"When Jesus grew up and started teaching, it was like nothing the people had heard before. Rabbis taught by quoting other rabbis to establish their credibility, much like professors do today. But Jesus spoke with a completely different kind of authority. During the Sermon on the Mount, he only quoted others to prove they were wrong or incomplete! He started his own teaching with, 'Surely I tell you . . .' The crowds were amazed because he taught as one who had authority, unlike their rabbis. He was a master teacher. Catching the picture?"

He nodded.

"So, then, what is his gospel?" she asked.

Uh-oh, he thought. He sensed a trap being set for him. But he ventured out anyway. If he was the hunted and the professor was the hunter, he knew she would ultimately be gentle. He bit hard on the bait.

"Well," he began. He put down his mug, flipped to an empty page on the professor's notepad and started to draw the familiar opposing cliffs separated by a chasm. "We all have sinned and fall short of God's glory. In our sin, we deserve death. But Jesus came to pay the penalty of our sins so that we can go to heaven when we die."

Shalandra grinned like a fisherman admiring her catch. "I know where you're going with this, and it's a start. But there's so much more. We said that Jesus was the master teacher. So what did he say the gospel was?"

Caleb raised his head and his eyes widened slightly. His mind was a blank. In all these years of being a Christian, he'd never once asked this question. Did Jesus even talk about the gospel? He must have: he was *in* the Gospels, right? But no biblical passage came to mind. He couldn't think of a time when Jesus gave a gospel summary, so he sat there stroking his chin, hoping something would come to him. His face started to feel flushed, and moisture gathered around his collar.

"I don't know," he finally said, weakly.

"And you call yourself a Christian?" she teased. But when he didn't smile back, she said, "Don't be embarrassed. It's surprising how many people don't know how to describe what Jesus said about the gospel."

He tried to smile, but if he were a cartoon, his head would've turned into a donkey's. He managed to keep himself from braying.

EMPIRE

"First," said Shalandra, "we need to enter Jesus' time and world. He grew up in a time of exile and expectation. In terms of exile, the pagan Romans ruled over the Jewish people, who thought they were the people of God. For them, it was just like when they'd been in exile many centuries earlier, captives in the pagan land of Babylon. And in that time and in Jesus' time, they longed for a new king who would establish a new kingdom. In terms of expectation, they hoped and longed for a new holy nation where all things were made right."

"Exile and expectation," he repeated.

"Jesus in particular grew up with Galileans, who weren't the backwater people we think they are. They were the most religious Jews of the time, and more famous rabbis came out of Galilee than anywhere else. Thus they zealously resisted pagan influences, so when the Jews revolted against the Roman Empire in A.D. 66 to 74, it makes sense that it started with the Galileans. They were known to stir things up — and Jesus was no exception. But he showed a different way than violent uprising."

Caleb could listen to this all day. Cultural background brought a greater richness to his understanding of the Bible. *When biology doesn't pan out,* he thought, *maybe I'll go to seminary.*

"So let's get to it," she said as she clapped her hands together. "What did Jesus call the gospel? Open up to Mark 1:14-15 and read it."

"After John was put in prison, Jesus went into Galilee, proclaiming the good news of God. 'The time has come,' he said. 'The kingdom of God is near. Repent and believe the good news!'"

"In Greek, the word for 'good news' is the same word for 'gospel': *euangelion,*" the professor said. "For Jesus, the gospel is 'the kingdom of God is near.' He doesn't say it any clearer anywhere else! The gospel is 'the kingdom of God is near!'" She stretched her arms wide open and beamed at him.

Caleb, however, stared back at her in silence. He knew he was supposed to be having a giant *aha!* moment, but it eluded him.

Shalandra backed up and tried to explain. "Let's process this a bit more. The word *gospel* meant something specific in Jesus' time. We use it as a religious word, but in his day it was a military word. Caesar, after conquering a region for the Roman Empire, would send messengers— the Greek word for angels—to spread the gospel."

She used her deepest voice: "You, new subjects of Rome! You don't need to worry about anything any longer. The Roman Empire has taken over the territory, bringing with it the *Pax Romana*—the peace and prosperity of Rome. You no longer need to worry about barbarians on your travel routes, foreigners invading your land, or a depressed economy—the Roman Empire will take care of all your needs. Caesar is lord and savior!"

"Did they actually say that back then?" asked Caleb. If so, then Jesus was really saying something seditious.

"Something very close. Caesar was lord and savior in his realm. This was the Roman gospel. But Jesus co-opted a military term and used it to announce his version of the *euangelion.* Since the Roman Empire was the dominant weave in the cultural fabric of Jesus' day, it makes sense that he would keep on borrowing words from the empire and twist them with new meaning."

So the word *gospel* described the message the Romans brought to their conquered territories? Angels were military messengers? And Jesus was using it here, in the outskirts of the empire, as if he'd reconquered the territory? No wonder the Jews wanted to hear him: perhaps he would be the new leader of the kingdom they hoped for.

"Wouldn't that be high treason?" he asked.

"You're catching on," she smiled, taking another sip of tea.

For Caleb it was easy to picture Jesus with a placid smile and a frail sheep around his shoulders, like chinchilla fur. Now he seemed like a revolutionary. A revolutionary Jesus without guns or steel but instead with love and sacrifice. Jesus didn't seem passive anymore, but more like a leader. A new kind of leader.

HEAVEN

"Okay," Shalandra said. "Now you know the gospel according to Jesus. But here's the bigger question: what is the kingdom of God?"

Caleb hoped it was a rhetorical question, but she kept waiting. He knew from their conversation so far that he probably had the wrong answer, but he couldn't think of another one in the moment. So he threw out the obvious.

"Heaven?" he ventured.

"Yes!" she said. Caleb was surprised—but her follow-up question shattered any sense of accomplishment.

"And what is heaven?" She waited again. She was taking her time with him today.

"Um . . . a place with God where we go when we die—if we believe," Caleb said, then stopped. By the sly smile on the professor's face he knew the trap had snapped again, closing tight around him. He could never get used to making mistakes in the open.

"Okay, it's a start," she replied as she sniffled. "Caleb, don't feel bad. But it's not the whole picture. The word *heaven* is pulled from Matthew's Gospel: he used the phrase 'kingdom of heaven,' presumably because he didn't want to offend his Jewish audience by using the word *God*. So heaven is actually the kingdom of God."

That made sense, sort of. He'd always thought the kingdom of God referred to heaven. But he knew he didn't fully grasp what the professor was saying.

"The phrase 'kingdom of God' was ripe with meaning for Jesus' audience," she continued. "It captured everything they hoped for. Expectation, remember? That's why he taught about the kingdom of God more than any other subject in the Bible. More than sin, sexuality, money, service, leadership, love. Hear where I'm coming from?"

"But you said they were waiting to overthrow the Roman Empire and start a new nation," Caleb said, a little frustrated. He felt like his head was a balloon and someone had forgotten to shut off the valve to the helium tank.

"Right!" she said. "But Jesus took a Roman word and Jewish expectations and infused them with deeper—even subversive—meaning. The Romans had the empire, and the Jews wanted to overthrow Rome. But Jesus' government wouldn't be built on Roman citizenship or Jewish heritage. It wouldn't even depend on the land it occupied. Rather, the kingdom of God would be the place where what happened was what God wanted to happen—regardless of land, culture, heritage or nationality. When people trust Jesus' way of life and live it out, that's where the kingdom of God exists. It's where Jesus really becomes king, not over land but over the hearts of people—and everything is made right."

"So instead of the kingdom of Israel that the Jews hoped for, Jesus ushered in the kingdom of heaven. 'The kingdom of God is near,'" he said, letting that truth sink in.

"Yes. And to live in this kingdom is eternal life—or better, the eternal kind of life. In the original language, the word translated as 'eternal life' literally means 'life in the age to come.' The word wasn't just meant to convey a life that was lived forever, like immortality, but to convey the kind of life that was *meant* for eternity. The kingdom kind of life. So the

old ways are gone, but new life has come. That's heaven—starting back
then and into forever. We enter into heaven, now and forever."

She then drew an inner circle with stick figures at the foot of the cross:

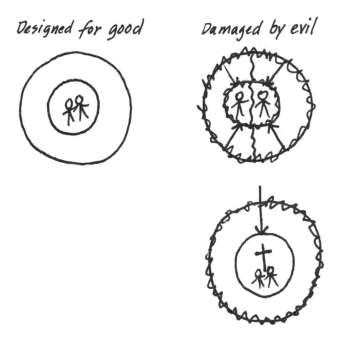

Her words took him by surprise, like a linebacker tackling hard from
his blind side. He was trying to get back up and stay in the game.

"Wait. So then, you're saying we live in heaven now?" He couldn't
believe what he was asking.

"Right! We don't just wait for heaven when we die, but instead it
rushes around us." She waved her hands around as she said this. "We
usher in heaven wherever we walk, whether in the classroom or the cubicle. Wherever we walk, the heavens rush around us."

Heaven—not just when we die? Heaven was something around us
now? Caleb unconsciously copied Shalandra's movements, grabbing at
the air around him.

"The heavens rush around us," he said. He sounded stupid just re-peating the professor, but he couldn't help it.

"Right! And here's one more twist. For the Jewish people, the temple was God's dwelling, the place of his presence—where heaven intersected earth. But Jesus redefined even the temple: it was no longer a building but his body. His body being the temple, it was now where heaven inter-sected earth. Are you following me? So when Paul turned it around again and said that *we* are his body, then guess where heaven intersects earth? Right—in the community of believers. That's where God's presence is supposed to be—and where heaven shows up on the planet."

Shalandra continued. "The kingdom of God is not supposed to be in some nation or government, but where the people who trust and follow Jesus are gathered. That's where heaven is. The kingdom of God is 'on earth as it is in heaven' when the poor are fed, the naked are clothed, the sick are healed, relationships—with nations, with us, with God—are all repaired. It's here. It's all around us."

All around us. Caleb knew God's presence was all around him and in him. And he knew that heaven was where God's presence was at its fullest. He just never put the two together. Doing so now proved to be powerful. The heaven he wished for after death had actually begun on this side of death. Heaven had already begun.

"So," Caleb said, "people in Jesus' time would have thought about heaven as where God is—his presence. And heaven after death is where we'll know God's presence fully. And in the end of time, we'll see the fullness of heaven—where the kingdom of God reigns over every part of the planet." Like all the king's horses and all the king's men, he was trying to put his theology back together again.

She nodded, smiling. He was catching on, but he felt like an old wineskin, and she kept pouring in the new wine. He hoped he wouldn't burst.

"So what's the good news about this kingdom of God?" Shalandra asked. "Jesus' gospel hinges on two verbs: 'has come' and 'is near.' The first is about time—an appointed time, a 'promised' time in the Greek, the time the people have been waiting for. The good news is that it *has come:* at the start of Jesus' ministry. The kingdom has come because the king has come. The second is about space—the kingdom of God is near. Heaven is so close you can touch it. So when you put those verbs together, the impact of this good news comes alive: the kingdom of God that you've been waiting for has already come, and you can now be a part of it. It's not by and by, but here and now."

"Before the cross and resurrection?" asked Caleb.

"Right; Jesus' invitation is before the cross. Now, the cross and resurrection are extremely important—"

"But how can it happen before the cross and resurrection?" Caleb interrupted. "You don't think they mean anything?" He didn't mean to be accusatory, but he was agitated. Was she going to make the cross and resurrection irrelevant as well?

But Shalandra kept her stride. "Like I said, they're absolutely vital. But they mean even more than just one thing. Lots of atonement theories exist out there. And I'm not just talking about heretical ones. You're used to one version, but there are others. In the earliest one in history, Satan holds humankind hostage because of their rebellion. But God tricks Satan into taking Jesus as a ransom for humankind. That's what theologians call it: the ransom theory. Satan accepts the deal, releasing humankind and killing Jesus. He thinks he's won, but Jesus comes back to life. So God gets both his son and his created people back.

"There are others, but the main point is that Jesus' death and resurrection are of the utmost importance. I like what Paul says: we are united with Christ. Everything bent and wrong with us dies with him. That's what the Bible calls our old selves. But everything that's right comes back to life in him, our new selves. And so each day we get a chance to pick up our crosses so we can truly live resurrected lives each day. Only Jesus can offer that. Another way to look at the cross is as something participatory, an invitation to a new kind of life—a kingdom kind of life. Each day, we sacrificially give of ourselves, loving others, possibly even to death."

Multiple theories on atonement? But which one was the right one? Caleb felt like one of Jesus' disciples when he told them to eat his body and drink his blood: this teaching was beginning to be too hard to bear.

"Can you show me the Bible passages?" he asked. And she did, taking her time with each one. The pieces did make sense, but it was all so new for him. "So, this is one way to look at it, right?"

"Yes," she said. "And there are others. The work of the cross is way too big to be explained by one theory. Each of these theories may have some truth in it and point to the significance of what Jesus did on the cross. But it's in the blend of these ideas that we get a fuller picture of the cosmic work of the cross. I choose a simple version, but all of them are worth studying."

"Would you show me the others?"

They took a long time looking at various interpretations of the work of the cross: as placating God's anger, as paying for someone else's legal punishment, as buying back a slave to freedom, as reconciliation between family members. Caleb made another mental note—*study atonement theories*—and continued to listen.

CHANGE

Shalandra sneezed. "Bless you," Caleb said.

"Thanks," she replied as she reached for a tissue. "Now, how does Jesus want us to respond to his gospel? He said to repent and believe the good news. So there are two responses. First, repent. We think of this as a religious word, of a Monty Python sketch where depressed monks are beating their heads with oversized Bibles." She laughed. "But again, this word wasn't a religious word. In the original language, the word for 'repent' literally means to have a 'change of mind.' It's changing your whole way of thinking or giving up your agenda. In A.D. 66, a Jewish historian named Josephus confronted a rebel leader who sought a violent revolt against Rome. He was from Galilee, no less. Josephus asked him to repent—to change his mind about the revolt—and believe in him and the Jewish aristocracy to work something out with the Romans."

Repent had a different meaning too? he thought.

"Second, to believe is more than to give mental assent. The verb means to place your trust in. Every time you see the word *believe* in the Bible, keep this meaning in mind—to place your trust in. There's a huge difference between belief and trust in English—belief is something you think is true, like water is made up of atoms in a structure we designate as H_2O. We believe it to be true, but it doesn't necessarily change our lives. Trust, on the other hand, changes our lives. We act on our new revelations. In an old analogy, a person says he can carry another person on his back and walk across a tightrope over Niagara Falls. Belief says, 'Yes, you can do it,' while trust says, 'I'll get on your back!'"

Caleb wasn't catching everything, but even the disparate blocks pointed to a conclusion: what he'd thought was the gospel before wasn't the whole picture. That scared him. Questioning his faith was one thing, but embracing a seemingly new truth was a completely different matter.

"So what were they to trust?" the professor continued. "The good news. Instead of the *Pax Romana,* Jesus was asking people to switch allegiances to this new nation—seek first the kingdom of God and his justice and all these things will be added to you as well. Not the Roman Empire but the kingdom of God. It was a new message, and it was absolutely subversive and dangerous."

"Shouldn't that be righteousness instead of justice, professor?" asked Caleb. Somehow he caught this, and he wasn't showing off—he really wanted to know.

"Good catch, Caleb," she said. "Yes, *righteousness* is a good word, but we have changed its meaning today. When we hear 'righteousness,' we hear 'personal holiness and character.' But that wasn't its only meaning for Jesus. The word also refers to justice—not the angry kind, but the kind where everyone is treated fairly. It's the Hebrew idea of shalom—peace for all, right relationships for all, justice for all. More than righteousness it's about righteousness all around . . ."

WINESKIN

Caleb suddenly waved his arms, like he was trying to get the attention of a driver careening out of control. "Hold on," he said. "Everything sounds like it's about the here and now. But I want to know: does the gospel talk at all about where I go when I die?" He pointed to himself for emphasis, and he didn't realize that he was breathing heavily.

"Sure, but it's not just about you," Shalandra said. "Read Colossians 1:19-20."

Caleb flipped over to Colossians. "For God was pleased to have all his fullness dwell in him, and through him to reconcile to himself all things, whether things on earth or things in heaven, by making peace through his blood, shed on the cross."

"See? Jesus died so that all things, whether on earth or in heaven—all things—would be reconciled to him. This is not just people, but also relationships and families and communities. People can forgive each other and be forgiven and live as if all has been made right—they can be reconciled to each other. But systems and anything else in creation can also be redeemed and reconciled."

She listed off the things as she thought of them: "Movies, music, art, rap, dance, poetry, comedy, literature, governments, politics, culture, money—Jesus died for all of it, and all of it can be restored and reconciled back to God. Anything that was used for another allegiance can be realigned for God's good purposes. God was not just saving the people in the world, he was saving the world itself as well."

Then she wrote the words "Restored for better" over that circle:

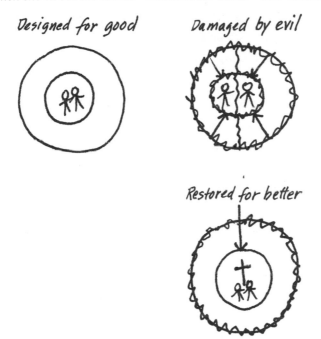

Designed for good   *Damaged by evil*

Restored for better

"But didn't Jesus save me?" his voice trembling. Though he liked what he heard, he was getting desperate.

"Well," she said with some hesitation, "yes—and far more. He not only saves us but the world. 'Salvation' in the original language also means 'deliverance' or 'healing.' So we've been saved-delivered-healed from our sins, are being saved-delivered-healed from our sins and will one day be finally saved-delivered-healed from our sins. So he saved you not only from eternal punishment, but also from the destruction your sin is causing you and the evil your sin is leading you into. Yes, he saved you—but not only from the punishment of your sins. He also saved you *from* your sins, and from sin itself. And he did this not only for you, but for the entire world."

"What do you mean by the world?"

She drew herself up. "I mean that Jesus didn't just save you and me. He saved-delivered-healed our relationships. He's doing the same with systems around us, like racism and materialism. He wants to do that with nations, governments, schools, churches, cultures. All of it can be restored for better."

On one hand, this new message answered his questions with the elegance Caleb had come to expect from the Bible. And sure, he had learned the past, present and future tenses of salvation before. But salvation as healing or deliverance? Multiple theories of the cross? Death and resurrection not only for a person, but also for the world? Reclaimed meanings for the words *repent, believe, heaven, gospel* and even *angel?* All of this felt too new. What about the faith he had growing up? Was that now all invalid? He knew that couldn't be the case either. So what was true here? What was reality? Would the real gospel please stand up?

"So what I've believe so far isn't true . . ."

Shalandra said, "No, it *is* true, but it isn't complete. You believed in a part, but Jesus wants us to embrace so much more."

Caleb, however, didn't hear her. Instead the wineskin burst. An awkward amount of time passed. His pen fell to the floor. He couldn't accept anymore. His thoughts were swimming through mud.

He grabbed the sides of his chair and slowly pushed himself up. He didn't meet the professor's surprised gaze. As if he were in a trance, everything faded—there was no professor, no books, no chairs. He turned around without saying a word and grabbed his coat. He pulled it on and walked out of the office. He didn't hear the professor calling his name or see the worried look on her face. He walked out through the front doors of the building and stepped into the rain.

HOLY

Caleb slowly shuffled across campus. The glue that held his thoughts together had melted away. He faintly heard someone say, "Hey! Watch
it!" as a student sloshed by on his bike, barely avoiding a head-on
collision.

He got into his car without shaking off the rain and drove home. His
mom said hello as he took off his shoes, but he ignored her and went up
to his room. He closed the door and lay down on his bed, not even bothering to get under the covers.

When he woke up, he looked at the illuminated bedside clock and
saw that it was a little after nine. He sat up and immediately thought
back to the conversation he'd had with the professor. If what she was
saying was true, then everything in his faith could be questioned. Yes,
the professor was right: she did take a wrecking ball to his faith. The
roof, the attic, the ceilings, the walls, the doors and the windows—
nothing was impervious to its swing.

He sat up suddenly, his eyes wide in the darkness. He remembered
that Shalandra had also said he had a foundation: Jesus. With all of the
demolition, Jesus was still, in Anna's words, cool. But now Jesus
seemed bigger and more relevant, and he was doing something revolu-

tionary for the planet. When he dug down deep, he found that Jesus was absolutely trustworthy, even in the midst of his internal chaos. He didn't know what his faith's expression would look like after this, but he knew that he loved and trusted Jesus even more than he had before. And he knew Jesus was still worthy of worship—again, even more so than he'd previously realized.

Caleb got out of bed and knelt quietly. He folded his hands and laid them on his bed, and he closed his eyes. He waited. The air seemed to become thick, and his skin bristled with electricity. Even the ends of his hair buzzed; it was as if a lightning storm was brewing around him in the darkness. Any sense of normalcy was sucked out of the room: the space had been made holy and he felt lucky that his shoes were already off.

"Jesus," Caleb said aloud, quietly but intensely, "you know the struggle I've been going through in the past few months. You know that I want to follow you, and I want to make my life's purpose all about you. I trust you. More than ever, I trust you. But I need you right now—"

His voice broke and his eyes started to fill. "I can't figure any of this stuff out. I thought I knew your message through and through. Now I realize I don't know much of anything. I'm lost. I don't know what's up or down, what's false or true. But I do know that you're good, and I still want to follow you, Jesus."

He knew someone was listening.

"Jesus, I'm really excited. But I'm scared. So lead me down the right path. If I learn something that is not of you, please let me forget it quickly. Let it be as far as the east is from the west. But if something is from you and it's just hard to swallow at first, please keep it in my mind and heart and show me your ways. Jesus, I need you right now. Please lead me. I need you. I need you . . ."

He let the tears flow down his cheek. He stayed on his knees for a few more minutes. He didn't want this time to end. He waited and listened. And then he heard a voice. No, actually, it was more like a hunch or an impression—but more than that, too. He couldn't quite place what it was, but he knew what the voice said: "I will be with you."

Now the sobs came freely, and his hunched shoulders shook. Snot, sniffles and prayers flowed together—a seemingly unholy combination that was utterly sacred. His heart felt like it would burst with gratitude. He started to pray fervently, his mouth uttering a torrent of praise and worship while he pounded the sheets—he prayed like his parents used to pray. And he kept on for at least an hour. Afterward, when the pressure within his heart had died down, he just felt stillness. Peace had entered. Shalom had arrived.

Caleb smiled for more than a few moments, took a deep breath and then pulled out his phone. He pressed the number three button for a while. Dave answered on the other end.

MOVEMENT

Anna and Caleb continued their walk down Memorial Way, heading for the flagpole and ultimately the underground parking lot. In the middle of all this history stood a modern blight: the law school, which looked like an overgrown greenhouse. It made you wish that people in glass houses did throw stones.

"Heaven is so much more than the afterlife," said Caleb, knowing how much he'd struggled to receive this message as good news. "Or perhaps more accurately, the kingdom of God is so much more. A kingdom back then was a lot like what a nation is to us today—a place where a ruler's wishes are carried out. In America's case, it's our government. Back in Jesus' time, it was Caesar's Roman government. In that context, Jesus came to start a new nation. He started a revolution and gathered a resistance movement. But it wouldn't be with violent overthrow, but a nation of true, intimate love and service to all people."

"You're starting to sound like a communist," Anna joked, trying to get a reaction out of him.

He smiled but answered her seriously. "I don't think I would put a political label on it. It was a new way of living, a new way of relating and a new way of organizing. Jesus, as the leader of this resistance movement, was calling his people to recruit others to live in this new way—where people live right lives, where they have right relationships and where they promote right systems so everyone and everything gets a fair shake. Shalom. Or where God's presence is—heaven. So heaven is all around us, and we're invited to be a part of it."

"It's a utopian theory," she said.

"Not quite. This one is grounded in reality instead of a novel in some author's imagination. Look at all the major social movements of the past two thousand years. Stuff like public education, higher education, literacy, children's rights, abolition of slavery, human rights, civil rights, women's suffrage—who started all of these movements? Christians."

"Hold on." Anna lost her smirk. "Don't give me that crap. Christians have been killing innocent people since the Crusades and the Inquisition." She was speaking quickly now. "The Pilgrims—God-fearers all, right?—gave their Indian neighbors blankets used by smallpox victims. Or what about the Conquistadores and what they did to Aztec and Incan empires? Those Spaniards brought guns and germs, all In the name of Jesus and converting the so-called heathen. Christians have done some jacked-up things, Caleb."

"I know, I know," said Caleb quickly yet softly, raising his hands in surrender. "We did do all that. And I'm not saying it was right. I'm sorry for what we've done. We did do some messed-up things in Jesus' name. But I can honestly say that Jesus wept too when those things were happening. They were done in his name, but he would never have approved. I hope we've learned from those things, but sometimes we keep on doing the same old things."

"Like the religious right," she shot back, pointing up at the American flag.

Ouch. "I don't know if that's fair, Anna—but I'm sorry that even Christians today sometimes don't do a good job of reflecting Jesus. But even though Christians have done all of that horrible stuff, so have other people. That's what all people have in common: we're capable of great evil. But at the same time, I think Christians get the short stick in the media and history books as well. They sometimes do a lot of good. So I just wanted to balance things out."

She crossed her arms but didn't say anything more, so he went on. "But look at communism. It's clearly an anti-religious movement—didn't Marx say that 'religion is the opiate of the masses'? But Stalin and Mao killed a hundred million people! That's way more than Christianity ever did. And think of the millions who died in secular wars like World War II. Might've done better to smoke more of that opiate, don't you think? In fact, 160,000 Christians die every year because of their faith. Christians are now on the persecuted end."

Anna sat quietly, and Caleb couldn't tell if she was curious or furious. She looked like she might want to chew Caleb out—yet he could tell she was hearing ideas she'd never encountered before. But then she apparently thought of something else.

"What about Gandhi—and nonviolent resistance? Isn't that Hindu?" she asked.

"Gandhi greatly admired Jesus and learned many of his principles of nonviolence from the Sermon on the Mount. But he hated what passed for Christianity in the West—like you. So even with Gandhi, nonviolent resistance was, at least in part, a Christian idea. We can look at some recent historical figures too. Martin Luther King Jr., Cardinal Jaime Sin, Oscar Romero, even Bono. They were people of faith who influenced governments and society—even the hearts of their oppressors—for better without violence."

Anna still had her arms crossed, daring him to continue.

CENTER

Lord, please help, Caleb prayed in his mind.

"Okay, Anna," he said. "Let's get back to Jesus."

"Good idea," she said smartly.

He recalled the third circle in the professor's diagram. "Jesus started his resistance movement to restore the world for better. But he had to do it a certain way. Instead of violent overthrow and killing others, he let his enemies kill him. If this world was diseased by evil and sin, then Jesus went right into the center of it and took it all onto himself. He died brutally. And in death he invited us to put to death the evil in us. All evil and its consequences died with Jesus on the cross. The Bible says we die with Jesus."

"We die?" she asked, eyeing him suspiciously.

"Yes. But Jesus came back to life three days later. He overcame evil and death no longer held him. So if we died with him, we also live a new life in him. We were resurrected with him. Jesus died the death we were already dying to give us the life we could not live on our own. He lives. And in that resurrection he proves that he's got the antidote to our disease. Think about it like this. There are two kinds of immunization: in active immunization, you're given a smaller version of the disease so your body can produce antibodies over time. But if it's urgent and life-threatening, you can also receive passive immunization, where actual antibodies are injected in your body. Jesus does that with us. He injects us with immunity to inoculate us from sin and evil. Our old ways are gone and the new has come. We are forgiven and the transformation has begun."

"We die and live in Jesus?" Anna was skeptical. "Come on, man. What does that mean? Obviously you're still alive, and you're not a remote-controlled robot operated by Jesus."

"Right. He doesn't control me because he loves me too much. He still wants me to figure out how to develop my own antibodies, through his presence. Each day we have the chance to die with Jesus—all the crap that keeps us from loving our neighbors can really go away. And each day we can live in Jesus; he helps us be the kind of good we want to see on the planet. We are being invited into Jesus' death and resurrection so we can die to our evil selves and live a new life—forgiven and loved. We trust Jesus in death, knowing we can trust him in life. He's our teacher and we follow his ways. And thus we start living in the kingdom of God—heaven rushes with us. We usher in heaven and its mercy and justice wherever we walk."

Anna's arms relaxed, but she still had questions. "Well what about life now? If Christians really did this, the world would be a different place, right? But Christians don't seem as immune to doing wrong as you say they are. You talk about a utopia, but the world doesn't look like that at all!"

"Great question," he said.

PART FOUR

Sent Together to Heal

BATTLE

Anna and Caleb reached the entrance at Odie and stood in front of the elevators that led to the underground parking lot. They weren't alone: a small group of students also waited around them, making for cramped quarters. Caleb wanted to continue their conversation, but it was drowned out by the crowded silence.

The elevator doors opened and they climbed in. The students ignored each other, trying to look busy staring at the elevator lights. When the doors opened to Anna's floor, the garaged air swooshed in. Caleb stepped out and took a deep breath, but he got a lungful of carbon monoxide. He coughed, and for a moment it seemed awkward to pick up the conversation again.

They had talked for a while now, first at de Lune and then along Memorial Way, so to push the conversation at this point felt risky. In jazz, if the musicians improvise one last time through the tune, the result can be inspirational or just plain tired. But right now the music was demanding that he keep playing.

"Okay, where were we?" he started. He couldn't think of a better segue, but Anna didn't miss a beat.

"The stuff about now," she said as they walked to her car.

"Right," said Caleb, relieved. "In this big story, there's a happy ending: one day, Jesus' resistance movement of love and justice will replace all other competing nations and governments and systems. All people will acknowledge Jesus' kingdom as the real, true one. This is heaven at its fullest, at the end of all time." His arms opened wide to suggest the scope of what he was saying.

"But what about now?" asked Anna, an edge in her voice. This was the third time she'd asked.

"Now we live in between those times," Caleb said, "between the start and finish of the restoration project. It's like we're in the middle of a construction project and we know what it'll look like in the end, but we're still dealing with the rafters, the wiring, the buttresses, the rubble—the mess. The resistance has started, but revolution isn't complete. So evil still exists, injustice still happens, racism still works its evil through societies, oppression still continues. But we've also got glimmers of hope and places of victory, like some of the victories we have made so far in helping people get human rights, civil rights and so on."

"But if we're in between times, how can we be so sure of the future?" she asked.

"Here's an analogy I've heard: at the end of World War II, the Allied forces stormed the beaches at Normandy. Though there were heavy casualties, it was the decisive battle of the war. The Allies knew that they'd essentially won the war after that day. It's called D-Day. But skirmish battles still occurred, and the war wasn't officially over. It wasn't until V-Day—Victory Day—that the fighting ceased in earnest. The Axis surrendered, and peace was brought back to the land. So we're in between D-Day and V-Day. D-Day for us is Jesus' death and resurrection. V-Day is when he comes back in the future and establishes his new nation. In the end he'll reward those who have been agents of the resistance movement of love and healing, and those who opposed it will find themselves at the receiving end of justice."

Anna nodded, taking it in. Caleb's ideas didn't ignore the junk on the planet, and they called people to action against it. And in the end, justice would reign. It was something she dared not hope for and yet needed to hope for.

"So," she said, putting things together in her own mind, "the cross and resurrection were important because that's our D-Day. According to you, the war's already won, but we still fight these skirmishes along the way."

"You got it! But I don't mean to paint those skirmishes as small. They're huge: violence, injustice and oppression still exist, but we're still waging war against it. It can sometimes feel like we're losing in the moment, but one day, all things will be made right."

"So we fight for justice in the meantime?" said Anna. "I don't mind that at all."

HATE

They stopped in the middle of a row of cars, by Anna's old red Sentra. She put her bag in the trunk but didn't close it.

"In the meantime," Caleb said, "we all have our orders from Jesus to be sent out as operatives of justice healing. We're being sent out together to heal this broken planet. Lots of Christians don't understand this and remain on the sidelines. But we don't go out in a paternalistic or imperialistic way either; we go in love and service. It's our role to make this world a better place. We start within ourselves, letting Jesus take the lead of our lives, training ourselves so that we're the kinds of people we wish to meet someday. We become the kinds of people who can—by the leading of God—do good instead of evil, to love instead of hate, who forgive instead of perpetrating injustice."

Anna appreciated how Caleb put himself on the witness stand: he included himself as one of those Christians who had sat on the sidelines waiting for their chance to get into heaven. But she had to look at herself as well: she fought for justice, often with good reasons when she started, but she often ended up in anger and impatience. She'd thought these were good things. So did her friends. The anger fueled them, gave them energy to really do something. But now she wondered if they were really accomplishing what they'd hoped for. Could she, as Caleb said, *become* the kind of good that they wanted to see on the planet?

Caleb continued. "Then we work on our relationships so they're places of healing, love and forgiveness instead of places where we hold grudges and contempt. We need to admit our wrongs to others and forgive others who have wronged us."

"Forgive others?" Her eyes burned.

"Yeah," said Caleb. "Jesus made this a huge point. If you don't forgive others, then your actions show that you aren't forgiven. To be agents in this revolution of love and service, he needs us to let go of our anger and bitterness so it doesn't take over. Otherwise our bitterness will bleed into our service."

"But—what if I can't?" she asked. There was no smirk, no sarcasm.

"What do you mean?" Caleb asked, and he waited. Even a place as musty and mundane as an underground parking lot could be reclaimed in Jesus' kingdom.

Anna paused for a long while, thinking hard. She crossed her arms and looked down, defiant yet helpless, searching for something to say. An SUV drove by.

"I can't forgive my dad, Cay," she finally said.

He just listened.

"Never mind," she said. But her lip started to tremble, and then a tear trickled down her cheek. Anna didn't like to talk about this: she'd told her counselor once about it and felt stupid crying in the office like that. Her father shouldn't still have power over her. She had built her castle and lived in it, impervious to slings and arrows from the outside, protected by brick and mortar and moat.

"Damn it, Cay," she wiped a tear away. She paused for a while, trying to collect herself. She let out a long sigh. Then paused some more.

Caleb kept silent, not knowing what to say and knowing that anything he said wouldn't help.

Then she steeled herself. "I hate him!" she said and she threw her fists out. "I've gone to counseling, talked to therapists, and I even tried writing him a letter to get some damned closure. But I still hate him. I can't forgive him. I won't forgive him. For what he did to my mom. To me. To my sister. I want him to burn in hell for what he's done to us!" With cold fury in her eyes she said, "I will never, ever forgive him. Ever."

She dared Caleb to say anything as tears streamed down her cheeks.

Caleb didn't know what to say. So he went with his instincts and stepped up to put his arms around her. But she shoved hard, pushing him away. She quickly wiped away her tears, slammed the trunk shut, and got into the car, closing the door behind her. Then she backed up the car aggressively and peeled away. The squeals from her tires echoed against the walls.

Caleb stood there, his face flushed. He prayed, "Be with her, Father. Be with her." But then he also couldn't help but turn his thoughts to himself: *I'm an idiot.*

PENANCE

Less than a year ago, Caleb had also been waiting for the elevators, except this time back at Padelford Hall. He nervously tapped his feet. He had already sent Professor Jones an apology for his crazy episode the previous week, explaining all that he had gone through in a lengthy e-mail. She had been gracious in return, but he still felt nervous. It was one thing to know that things would be okay and another thing to feel it. To make amends he'd brought the ultimate Seattle peace offering: two cups of mocha latte steamed in his hands.

He entered the office with his head penitently bowed, lattes extended. When the professor saw him, she shot up and gave him a big hug, like she was greeting someone she hadn't seen in a long time. Perhaps that was right: he felt like a different person. He threw his hands outward, trying to receive the hug while balancing the cups. When the professor noticed the awkward position she'd put him in, she let go and laughed hard. Then she took the cups from his hands and put them on her desk—all in one motion, like a ballerina. She smiled and hugged him again, and he felt forgiven.

"So, are you okay?" she asked, staring straight into his eyes like a doctor checking out her patient. She gave him a friendly shake by the shoulders.

"Yeah," he said, shrugging. "Like I wrote in the e-mail, I was just trying to soak it all in. I'm really, really sorry. I'm really embarrassed."

"It's all right," she said comfortingly. "I admit, you had me worried. But don't worry. It's all good now."

"Thanks. I think I'm better now. It's strange, because it seems like the things I used to know I really didn't, but then I know more of what I did—does that make sense?"

She shook her head honestly. "Say that again?"

He grinned. "What I mean is—I thought I knew what the gospel was. Now I'm not so sure. But I know that Jesus is even bigger, smarter and cooler than I'd thought before. He really came to restore the whole world—and he's succeeded in so many ways. I know now less than ever, but I trust Jesus now more than ever. It's weird."

"That's wonderful—and normal," she said, nodding slowly. "When you question the things you used to know and then come to the beginning of some answers again, it somehow feels more real and more vibrant. Flannery O'Connor once wrote, 'Don't expect faith to clear things up for you. It's not about certainty, but about trust.' Sounds like that's where you're at."

In the past, having the right answers had felt like living at the zoo: it kept him safe, but it was like a dungeon. Admitting that he didn't have the answers was like having the bars and gates come crashing down and seeing that the verdant fields were not meant to be avoided but to be run through and played in.

"So, shall we continue?" said Shalandra.

"Sure—what's next?"

"Okay—Jesus started this new nation," she said, pulling out the now-familiar notepad and pen.

"Yeah," said Caleb. "I was thinking about that. If we're in heaven now, then what about all the junk in the world? There's plenty of places where what God wants to happen doesn't happen."

She didn't answer right away but drew another circle with jagged lines, an inner circle and a cross:

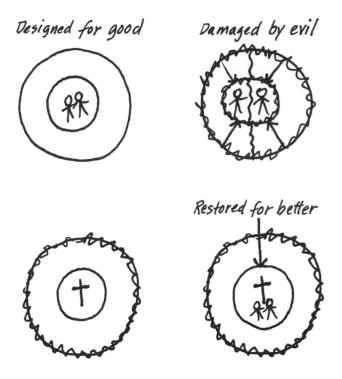

Designed for good   Damaged by evil

Restored for better

"Good point," she finally replied. "The fullness of heaven does not happen until the end of time, when history is finished. But in the meantime, we usher in heaven now—this kingdom goes forward with us. So we respond to the kingdom by being messengers and ambassadors to people and places that don't know or understand Jesus' rule and reign."

To Caleb, that made sense. People were supposed to be messengers—angels—themselves, blessing the planet and the people around them. Somehow, that was part of the good news as well, or at least part of the response to it.

"So, I've got another question," she said. "How do we become Christians?" She waited again: the long, painful wait.

Caleb knew what was going to happen. But he tried anyway. Smiling weakly he said, "Well, we accept Jesus' forgiveness for us and invite him to be in relationship with us. It's the start of a new relationship with Jesus, and we let him become the leader of our life."

"Good," she said. "A great answer." Caleb was relieved, but only for a moment.

"But is that all?"

MISSION

"Okay, let me approach this from another angle," she said. "How did Jesus invite people to be Christians?"

"Come follow me," he said instinctively. "Come follow me and I will make you fishers of men, right? Yes!" He couldn't help it: he threw his head back and his fists into the air, like he had won Olympic gold.

She grinned. "Good," she said. "Now think about that for a moment. When did Jesus' disciples become Christians? Before the resurrection? At Pentecost? It's a hard call, right? But check out what Jesus says. He could have said, 'Come follow me and I will make you feel at peace,' or 'Come follow me and I will make you more joyful than anything else you've ever experienced.' We invite people to faith this way—we tell them the benefits of following Jesus first. Now, these are real byproducts of following Jesus, but what is he calling them to?"

"Be fishers of men," Caleb said, catching on.

"Right. From the very outset, Jesus invites them to join in his mission—to advance the kingdom he started. From the get-go, Jesus gives them a picture of what it means to serve people and to stop seeking their own self-gratification. He wanted them to look up from the selfishness of their own hearts and to start serving others with love and justice.

Come follow me and I will," she paused again for emphasis, "make you fishers of people. We run over this verse quickly because it's so familiar, but Jesus is giving them a purpose from the very beginning."

How many times had Caleb read this passage? So often he was able to quote the words from memory at a moment's prompting, yet he never understood the impact of these words. Jesus didn't just make promises for his disciples, but he called them into a purpose that was larger than themselves. He called them into mission even before his death on the cross. He started to wonder what that would look like in the world today. How would he apply it? What if he invited his friends into a new purpose as Jesus did?

"Here's something else, and this will finish our Genesis study," the professor continued. "After all that crap that humans did to each other up to Genesis 11, God makes a pact with Abram in Genesis 12. Read Genesis 12:2-3 for me."

"'I will make you into a great nation, and I will bless you,'" Caleb read. "'I will make your name great, and you will be a blessing. I will bless those who bless you, and whoever curses you I will curse; and all peoples on earth will be blessed through you.' As someone God blessed, he was supposed to bless others!"

"Exactly. Abram was blessed to be a blessing. All peoples would be blessed through him. And the fullness of that promise would come through one of his descendents. You got it—Jesus. But Abram was supposed to be a blessing himself as well. And so are we. See, we've painted the Christian life too small. We've made it all about the individual—about my feelings, or the number of Bible passages I've read or prayer times I've had in a given week. We've made faith something internal instead of a blessing we offer externally. We've created a religion that's individualized, privatized and personal instead of public, communal and loving of others. We need to recapture the mission as a part of our gospel. For the Christian religion will be judged by the amount of blessing it brings to its outsiders."

Caleb's heart leapt at her last words. If Christianity was evaluated according to the amount of blessing it brought to its outsiders, how would it fare? A mixed report card, at best. Above average? Maybe. But Caleb hoped that it would one day receive high marks.

"Let's break this down further," Shalandra said. "What does it mean to be fishers of people? First, Jesus gets to be in charge. In this passage, he's proven that he can fish—his disciples catch a boatload. So we learn from the master. That's how we learn how to fish." She pointed to the inner circle to emphasize her point.

"Then we join his community of believers, because it's always about community. That's where heaven intersects earth, remember? The community is the new temple of God. I love that verse in Ecclesiastes: a cord of three strands is not quickly broken. There is strength in numbers, and it's also true in Christian community. We need each other, not only for our own sake but for the sake of the world."

Then she added four pairs of people into the diagram.

"Who's your community, professor?" asked Caleb. He really wanted to know. It was easy to put professors on a pedestal and not think about them as normal people.

Shalandra seemed surprised by the question but went along anyway. "Back in Boston I had a whole community of friends and mentors. I was there for college and stuck around for graduate school. These people helped me not give up on God after a bad breakup. I really thought

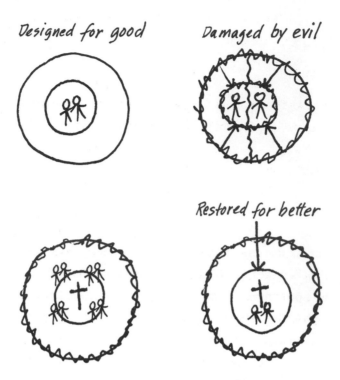

I was going to marry that man, as clearly as I knew that I was going to be a professor." She chuckled wistfully.

"So after the breakup I questioned everything, even my faith. My friends prayed with me, cried with me. I really wouldn't have made it without them. They encouraged me to take classes in theology, so I checked out seminary. It's funny; seminary never interested me until I started having questions. Other professors poured their lives and wisdom into me, and one of my pastors was like a second mom to me."

The professor paused and thought for a moment. "I still need community. I've got a great small group at my church. I can tell them anything. I know they really care about me. Together we try to be a community of healing for others. And sometimes I just need someone to tell me it's okay to be single—for now." She laughed, shaking her head.

Caleb felt his chest tighten slightly. He was grateful for his mentor. And he was thankful for friends like Dave and Tom. Faith couldn't be just about him. Community had to play a huge part. What good was it for him to be right but not have any friends with him in the fight? He needed community. Though it was tempting to worm backward into his own brain and construct a private world and universe to live in, he knew he needed the love of his friends.

"So we need to be in community," Shalandra said. "It supports us, yes. But it does much more than that. Christian community at its best is a taste of the kingdom of God. Paul takes this even further. In 1 Corinthians 12, he says we are the body of Christ. The community *is* Jesus to the world. Before, Jesus was only in Jerusalem and traveling around Judea. Now he's everywhere: Bangkok, Cairo, New York, London. You name it; he's there. How? Through us. His body is still on the planet, through us. In that way, community exists so that others know that Jesus exists. We are the body of Christ."

This was cool. Caleb had heard about the body of Christ before. Everyone at church talked about it. But usually they said that it meant that believers were connected. In this interpretation, Jesus was actually represented through his followers. *We are his body.*

"Not only do we have each other, but we also have someone greater," Shalandra said. "What is the biggest promise in the Bible?" Caleb knew the answer, but she didn't wait this time.

"More than great riches or perfect health, the main promise of the Bible from Genesis to Revelation is that God will be with us. He promised to be with Isaac, Jacob and Joseph. When Moses feared the Egyptians and when Joshua was about to invade the Promised Land, God said he would be with them. He said the same to Gideon when he was shuddering in a winepress hiding from his enemies. To Solomon and Jehoshaphat he said it again. Through Isaiah, God promised to be with *us*. Jesus said to his disciples that he would be with them always, until the very end of the age. God promises to be with us and he is with us—through the Holy Spirit."

God promises to be with us. Caleb smiled and remembered that night beside his bed. He'd stopped believing in mere coincidence a long time ago. So when Shalandra brought up this idea, he knew he truly wasn't alone. Someone out there was guiding him.

"The Holy Spirit lives inside of us," she continued. "And he gives us the kingdom resources we need to do the impossible—to live as if sin did not control us. The Spirit is our guide into the kingdom, and we are now citizens. He helps us along the way. And this Holy Spirit invites us

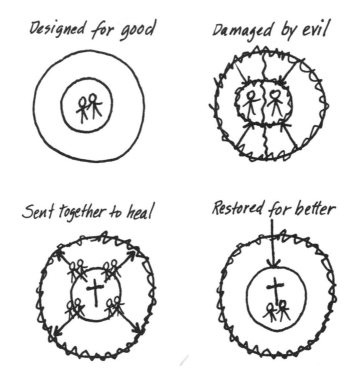

to be with other followers of Jesus—revolutionaries of Jesus, if you like. We cannot do this work alone. So God gives us resources, in his own presence through the Holy Spirit and also in his community of followers on the planet. That's what church is supposed to be, and I know we're not perfect, but we keep pressing on. Christians are sent out together to heal the planet with the Holy Spirit."

Shalandra drew four arrows radiating out from the inner circle, pressing up against the jagged edges of the world. Then she wrote the words "Sent together to heal" over the final circle.

"And that's it," she said. "Here's the gospel. What do you think?"

TREASURE

The sun was starting to set, casting a long golden glow over the professor's desk. Seattle at sunset was absolutely stunning if it wasn't raining. The yellow glow was like treasure gold, like a closing chest offering one last peek at the glory inside.

Caleb stared at the diagram and saw the entire scope of the Bible. The pictures captured more of the heart of the Scripture than anything he'd been taught before. He thought about what it would be like to share it, about how his friends would react. He brought up a question Anna would surely raise.

"What if you think you're in the fourth circle trying to heal the planet and you don't think you need the third circle? Why can't we just jump to the fourth circle without the third?"

"That's a great question, Caleb!" The professor beamed. "People identify with this particular diagram in many ways. Some people identify with the first circle, where they think life is fine and dandy. But then it doesn't match up to present-day reality—just take a look at the news. Some folks relate to the second circle, where they feel overwhelmed by the damage and evil in the world and have no idea what to do next. That's where Jesus provides a great solution."

This could be helpful, Caleb thought. Even if he didn't actually share the diagram, he could keep it in his mind and help people connect with the gospel.

"Or they could be the third circle, where they've accepted what Jesus has done for them but haven't partnered with God and aren't living out his purposes for the planet—the fourth circle," Shalandra said. "And if they're not in the fourth circle, they're not participating in the kingdom of God."

Yes! How many Christians just accepted what Jesus had done for them without jumping into the mission of the kingdom? It was scary to Caleb how many people had probably done just that, but if they all entered into the fourth circle, this world really could be a different place.

The professor pulled the notepad toward her and added a few more lines, drawing a diagonal chasm between the second and fourth circles with an arrow dead-ending in front of the chasm:

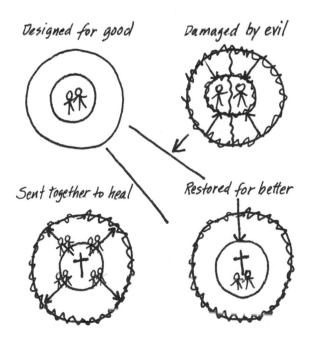

"Now back to your question," she said. "Some people think they're in the fourth circle but haven't gone through the third circle, and they don't want to. But if we try to change the world on our own resources, we're doomed to fail on every level." ⸗

She pointed to the arrow leading into the chasm. "We should never underestimate the power of evil. It's quite strong, and it's too easy for us to become jaded, burnt out, angry, apathetic or even corrupted ourselves. We need the Holy Spirit and the community of Jesus' followers to help us in the fight. We can't do it alone."

Shalandra went on. "More importantly, we need to become the kind of good that we want to see on the planet. We need to be transformed so we can take evil full on and not be corrupted by it. Because whatever we do, we can't hide our junk for long. No matter how much good we're trying to do, the faults of our character will press through the cracks of our masks. Over time, if left unchecked, my anger, impatience, judgmentalism, hatred, cynicism and despair will all seep through. And I'll be tempted to make the ends justify the means. We can't use evil tactics to bring about good. Instead, we learn to love instead of hate, give instead of take, persevere instead of giving up."

We need to be the kind of good we want to see on the planet, Caleb repeated in his mind. He didn't want to forget that phrase. Shalandra drew another set of arrows, leading from the second to the third, and from the third to the fourth circle.

"So, we need to go through Jesus. We let him take charge of our lives, and each day we submit ourselves to the Holy Spirit to help us be agents of healing and reconciliation to the planet. Basically, each day, we trust him. Jesus is the best way to deal with evil on the planet."

I could say this, he thought. It was a practical progression that made sense. Jesus did not exist only for the benefit of his own soul but

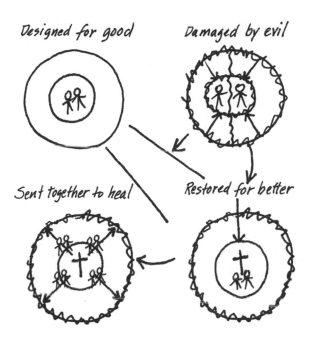

also for the sake of the entire world. And this sounded more and more like good news. But he was reminded of something that he didn't want to forget.

"Um, can I have that?" he asked, pointing to the diagram.

PRAYER

Caleb stood in the parking lot for a few minutes. His talk with Anna had been going so well. He didn't feel like fighting through traffic to get back home, so he went back upstairs to Odie. He looked for Dave and Tom; they were usually there. But he couldn't find them, and then he remembered his text message.

He pulled out his phone and read: *prayin 4 both of u. ttyl, dm.*

He knew that Dave had prayed for him and for his conversation with Anna. But he wished he'd prayed a little harder.

Caleb found a carrel on the second floor and plopped his backpack on the desk. At the very least, he should probably get some studying done.

REVERSE

Anna raced out of the garage in a heat of anger. *Who the hell does he think he is?* she thought furiously. She raced up Fifteenth Avenue and headed up I 5, but instead of speeding along on the freeway, she found herself immobilized by hundreds of other cars. *No, no, no!* She hit the steering wheel with both of her fists repeatedly. The last thing she wanted was to be stuck in traffic.

She aggressively changed lanes to the left, hoping to get some clearance, but there was nowhere to go. She inched along, speeding then braking, speeding then braking, making her car buck like a rodeo steer. She gave up the commute home and pulled off at the next exit and thought about heading to Green Lake. But she could see that the traffic was backed up mercilessly there as well, so instead she pulled back toward campus, thinking she might go to the University Village, a hip shopping area near campus, for some coffee. But the left she needed to take on Forty-Fifth was not allowed at this time of day. *What the hell was going on?*

Exasperated, Anna pulled her car over near the rear of the bookstore. She gripped the steering wheel hard with both hands and shook herself. Then she gave out a long, loud scream. Tears streamed down her cheeks. She covered her face with her hands and wept hard. She wept over the way things weren't supposed to be: with her dad, with her family, with herself.

After a few minutes, she stopped almost as suddenly as she started. She collected herself and took a few deep breaths. She looked into the rearview mirror, wiping away tears and runny makeup.

Then she picked up her phone and made a call. "Where are you?" She paused. "I'll be right there."

VOICE

Caleb was afraid to offer Anna a hug when they met at the library. She didn't volunteer one either. They sat in a corner lounge of the library, on a couple of square vinyl ottomans. Long floor-to-ceiling windows divided up the concrete walls and let in the waning natural light. They spoke in whispers.

"I'm glad you came back," he said.

"Didn't have a choice," she sulked. "Traffic was horrible."

Caleb couldn't help but think, *Thank you, Jesus.* "Are you okay?"

"Yeah—I am. Sorry back there. I guess I freaked. But I'm up for finishing what we started."

He was stunned at her openness but didn't want to miss the moment. The words tumbled out without thought or self-consciousness. "Okay, I want to tell you something. I think God is speaking to you." He stared unflinchingly into the depth of her eyes.

She didn't say anything and stared back, searching his face for meaning.

"Why else would you be back here?" he asked, his gaze never leaving hers.

"What do you mean? Does God speak to you, Cay?"

"Well," he said, searching for the words, "sort of. I mean, he does. I'm not saying he tells me what color my toothbrush needs to be or which direction to walk—though I don't count that out either."

He told her about how God had spoken that one phrase—"I will be with you"—in his bedroom and how it had been one of the most profound experiences of his life.

"Wow," she said. "You're really serious about this stuff."

"Yeah, and I think he's talking to you," he answered. Tentatively, he added, "And I think he's asking you to forgive your dad."

"But I really don't know how," she said plainly.

Caleb gulped and said, "Trust Jesus, and he'll help you. Let him take charge over your life. Let him know that you don't know how to forgive. That's an honest start. And he will help you. You'll have more power to forgive when you know you're forgiven. And then you'll have more resources to pursue love and justice with God's Spirit and with his followers, to restore the world back to its original design."

Forgiveness could change the planet? Anna thought about what he was saying for a moment. She was skeptical, and she must have looked it, because Caleb went on.

"It happened in South Africa with the Truth and Reconciliation Commission," he said. "Bishop Desmond Tutu led a process with the approval of the South African government where any crimes would be forgiven if the perpetrator came forward and admitted his or her crimes in front of the victims. Both white and black people confessed and received forgiveness, and it healed a nation—without violence! Jesus' revolution at work."

Anna smiled wide and said, "You're trying to convert me, aren't you?"

"I'm not forcing you to do anything," Caleb said, trying to protect the solemnity of the moment. "But if God is speaking to you and asking you to give over the leadership of your life to him, what will you do? Will you give it over to him? Will you join his movement?"

"Well, what would that mean?"

TIME

"Okay. Here are three ideas I can think of," Caleb began.

He thought of the fourth circle in the diagram. "First, start to trust Jesus with your life. He gets to be in charge because his ways are best for us and for the world. Let him start to love you. Admit that we have contributed to the evil on the planet and that we need forgiveness. Receive Jesus' forgiveness and invite the Holy Spirit into your life. Then, join a community of people who are trying to follow Jesus and bring this new nation into reality. Find a group of Christians who can help you along in the journey, and meet with them regularly to get to know Jesus and be more like him."

"That'll be really hard," she said. "I remember what church was like."

"I know what you mean. Perhaps that church wasn't the best for you," he said. "My church right now has a few problems too—I guess they all do—but you could come with me."

"Maybe," she said, glancing away.

"Okay," he said, not wanting to press her too much. At least it wasn't a no. "Last, you ask God what he wants you to do next to advance his ways. Embrace the purpose that God has for you on the planet. What's great is that you're already doing so much that lines up with the kingdom of God. But you can ask him if there's anything else. Ask him to help you find what you should be doing next."

Anna was silent. Caleb wondered if she was thinking about her father. If all this stuff was true, she'd have to forgive him—and he knew it wouldn't be easy. But he didn't have anything more to explain. The time had come.

"So," he said as nonchalantly as he could, "how does this sound, this Jesus stuff?"

Anna looked down and rubbed her hands together. She breathed in, then back out again. Finally she said, "I'll think about it."

She got up and Caleb followed her. They went to the elevators and then out to her car. To his surprise, she turned and gave him a hug. He was glad to return it. And she pulled out, waving as she left. He prayed under his breath as she headed toward the exit.

EPILOGUE

New Beginnings?

BOBA

It had been more than two months since that eventful day at de Lune, and Caleb and Anna were just starting the spring quarter. It was early April, still the rainy season in Seattle, and April showers usually brought May . . . showers.

On this day, however, the weather was unusually sunny and gorgeous. All eyes blinked, squinted and ached at the newfound burst of ultraviolet. The cherry blossoms in the quad were in full bloom, like pink clouds. You almost expected the birds to break out in song. But Shalandra didn't catch the beauty right then.

She choked on a tapioca ball.

"What is this?" she asked, looking down into her cup in horror.

"Boba," Caleb replied. After finding out that Professor Jones hadn't even heard of bubble tea, he decided to take her out to Mitsu's and introduce her to his favorite drink. They were sitting at the window bar, swapping stories about what they'd each done during the break. "It's milk tea with tapioca balls at the bottom. They're called boba. You chew them while you drink. Ain't it great?"

Professor Jones took another sip, and was surprised again by the four tapioca balls that shot up through the wide pinstriped straw like bullets. After she chewed, she said, "I'm not sure I'll ever get used to this."

Caleb slurped his drink. It had been a year and a half since they started hanging out, and he still had many questions. But he was more hopeful and energetic than he'd been a year ago, and he owed much thanks to the wise counsel of his friend. These days he still came by her office, and once in a while he'd pick her brain on some theological subject that was bothering him. But more often than not the visits were social—their conversations focused on personal matters, and he received her prayers of wisdom and discernment.

"So," she asked slowly, giving him a mischievous look. "Anything else new?"

He looked to the ceiling and responded, "Oh, not much."

"Oh, really?" she said, taking another slurp of boba. She'd taught enough classes not to be afraid of silence. But it was too much for Caleb.

"All right, I give in. It's about Anna again."

TENT

Later that day Caleb was in the middle of Red Square. Lots of people were out basking in the sunshine, but Caleb was tending a line of students that snaked out from a large canvas tent. They were willing to wait for an hour to enter it.

Soon after talking with Anna at de Lune, Caleb had set up another meeting with Pastor Jeff. This wasn't unusual—Caleb was still leading the worship team and they had to coordinate often. Jeff had already apologized for not listening the time before, and Caleb had felt his sincerity. In turn Caleb had apologized for being impatient. And with tears they embraced. Since then they had worked on rebuilding trust in their relationship, and though they still didn't see eye to eye on everything, it was a start.

What was unusual about this meeting was that Caleb had brought Dave and Tom with him. Dave sat to his right, his long body cramped in Jeff's small office. Tom was on his left, his round face all smiles.

"I've got an idea," Caleb said to Jeff. "Dave and Tom think it's a good idea, too."

"It's sick!" Tom said. He meant it as a compliment.

Caleb laid out the plan, which was based on something he'd experienced during a student missions conference. He'd walked through a large canvas tent listening to an electronic narrator tell the story of Sarah, an African teenager affected by the AIDS pandemic. Caleb literally walked through Sarah's life, entering into the hut where she lived, hearing the knock of a well-dressed man at her door, hearing her scream "No, no, no please!" as he rapes her, because he thinks sex with a virgin will cure AIDS. She's not only pregnant, but HIV-positive. It was a horrifying experience and opened his heart to the hurts of the world. This experience had been one of the major reasons he went to Manila.

"What if we brought the tent here for a week?" Caleb asked Pastor Jeff. "But instead of just telling the stories, we give people a chance to respond. We could raise money to build a health clinic, provide education and offer other services to fight AIDS in Zambia. At the end we can share the gospel too. People will need to process their feelings after the experience, and we can share why Jesus cares about this and what his people are doing about it. Then we can invite people to join in and be a part of his healing movement. What do you think?"

Pastor Jeff didn't miss a beat. "That's a great idea, bro! Did you say the tent's already made?"

"Yeah," Tom jumped in. "I gave the organization a call, and they said anyone can use it. We just have to give them the dates and pay for the shipping." Dave nodded his head and gave a thumbs-up sign.

"I think I can get this on the church budget," said Pastor Jeff. He held out his fist and tapped everyone else's. "Bros, this is going to be awesome."

But Caleb wasn't finished. "I'd like you to see something," he said to Jeff. "For the gospel presentation, can we try something like this?"

And he began drawing the diagram he'd learned in the professor's office.

SQUARE

When the next group was ready to enter the tent, Caleb ushered them into the first room where Anna was waiting. They had on matching brown T-shirts, along with everyone else hosting the tent. Anna explained step by step what people could expect throughout the tent and invited them to keep their hearts open to anything they might feel led to do. Caleb wrapped up, letting them know that someone at the end would help them process their experience, offer a short overview about why Jesus cared about this issue and provide steps to respond. Then they sent the group further in to receive their audio players. Dave and Tom were in there, happily assigning the newcomers their path: one of three stories of children affected by the AIDS pandemic.

Anna and Caleb came out of the tent, and Caleb marveled that people would wait so long for the experience. The *Daily* had run a front-page article about the tent. Twice. The campus administration loved the awareness they were bringing to the AIDS issue, which allowed them to be on Red Square in the first place. And the line would not quit: the tent was open twenty-four hours a day and the lines were even longer at night. At that point students were given lanterns to walk through, which added an other-worldly feel to the experience.

Pastor Jeff was outside with his arms crossed, admiring all the work his students had put into this project. He smiled and shook his head: he couldn't imagine this happening a year ago. But Caleb was helping him see the larger scope of the kingdom of God. It wasn't just about individuals, but about the world as well. And in it the church could be a blessing. He felt thankful that Caleb kept challenging him and didn't give up on him. Many college students would have after that awkward conversation.

He spotted Caleb and Anna, walked up and gave them both a side-hug. Caleb returned the hug, but Anna instinctively pulled away.

"Sorry," Pastor Jeff said sheepishly.

"Don't worry about it," she said. She would've been more upset if she didn't trust him. She had been attending Experience and liked most of what he had to say, especially the stuff on Jesus. She freaked out a little about the music—everyone looked so intense. But what spooked her even more was that at times she found herself in tears. During these episodes something tightened around her chest, something both frightening and comforting. It was as if beauty were trying to escape from her heart and run free, but she couldn't allow it—it would be too achingly glorious. It was something she'd never felt before. Was she becoming one of them? She had no idea, but the tears certainly flowed more freely these days.

After the services, she hung out with Caleb's friends. Tom and Dave seemed like good guys. They'd chill with a bunch of other people, and she was starting to feel comfortable.

Pastor Jeff left them to see how the follow-up at the end of the tent was doing. Caleb turned and gave Anna a hug, and this time she didn't pull away.

"Isn't this great?" he said.

"Definitely." She gave him a wink, which could've meant many different things, but it didn't matter. She enjoyed her time with him, and they spent lots of time together these days. She wondered when Caleb would ever bring up the "talk." He'd better . . .

Later, Caleb would honestly admit that he couldn't tell if it was the wink or something else that pressed breath and life and wonder into his chest, making him feel like he was about to burst. But, in it all, his heart felt strangely warmed.

Behind the Scenes—

The Big Story —

WHY WE NEED IT

This story's over, but the Big Story is still waiting to be shared.

Because good news is not meant to be held back. We're wired to tell someone about it. Whether it's a good book, an inspiring movie, a job promotion, a luxurious getaway, a catchy song, an exhilarating hike or a random encounter with an old friend, we really can't wait to grab someone and load them up with the details. Don't get me started about my newborn son.

So why is it so hard for us to share the greatest news in the history of humankind, the news that Jesus heals and restores our relationships with God, each other and the rest of the world? One possibility: it doesn't feel like good news to us and we worry that it won't sound like good news to our friends.

THE KINGDOM OF GOD IS NEAR

For centuries, open-hearted Christians have quoted this line: "In essentials, unity. In nonessentials, liberty. In all things, charity." It reflects Jesus' prayer for the future Christian community—he hoped they would be in complete unity so the world would know that God loved them and had sent Jesus as proof. It highlights the decision at the Jerusalem Council in Acts 15, which turned a fledgling Jewish sect into a welcoming faith for all ethnicities, cultures and nationalities. It honors Paul's repeated challenges to live in unity, even if the Christian community disagrees on controversial issues such as food sacrificed to idols, circumcision and the use of spiritual gifts.

But here's the rub: what's essential and what's not? The line between essential and nonessential has always been blurry, leading to strife, division and even violence among the followers of Jesus Christ. In the end, we're left with this question: what's really at the core of the gospel?

In one of the simplest—and therefore most popular—articulations of the gospel today, our sins have separated us from God and make us deserving of eternal punishment. But Jesus takes on the punishment himself so that our relationship with God can be restored. We enjoy eternal life, which we assume to be paradise after death, and have an individual relationship with God while on earth. This explanation, along with the bridge diagram that often accompanies it, is usually considered the encapsulation of our faith's central message.

This summary is easy to remember, and I've used it countless times. Back in college I would often ask my irreligious fraternity brothers if they wanted to hear the entire Bible explained in ten minutes. When one of them was curious or drunk enough, he'd let me share it. I'd spice it up with some personal stories about my own relationship with God, and when the Spirit blew our direction, a brother might make his first decision to follow Jesus. From these experiences I became addicted to ministry.

However, I hit a point where the gospel just didn't feel like good news anymore. In that season, when the ministry's yearly cycle slowed down enough so that I could think, I asked my good friends, "What is faith, anyway?" They tried their best to listen and help, but I wouldn't be placated. They graciously took the full brunt of my angst. Then we'd go play video games for hours to escape. I have great friends.

My problem? The gospel sounded arbitrary. In a marketplace of religions, where all roads are supposed to lead to the same truth, Christians can seem arrogant when they claim that Jesus is the only way. To me our gospel seemed intolerant and exclusive—two major no-no's in today's culture. All we could say was, "It's the truth." End of discussion. And listeners would basically respond, as Pilate did, "What is truth?" We couldn't prove anything. They had their truth; we had ours. No one had frequent flyer miles for traveling between this life and the afterlife to give us the real scoop (though some bestselling authors might say otherwise). By the time anyone really knows for sure, it's too late.

In the introduction to this book I mentioned a friend who said he would choose against heaven if it meant he couldn't be with his family. He'd choose hell with family over heaven without. Sure, we could say he was missing the point, but in a day when the main spiritual question is no longer "What is true?" but "What is real?" or "What is good?" the gospel as most of us have learned it doesn't sound like good news. At least it didn't to my friends. And if I was being honest, it didn't to me. My motivation for ministry waned. No matter how much I tried to numb the angst, the splinter in my brain remained.

A few years ago Dallas Willard took his theological tweezers and began to extract the splinter. I had the privilege of taking his class on spirituality and ministry, and he seemed to be saying revolutionary things. So much so that it was hard to swallow at first. But through Scripture, he explained that the gospel Jesus taught was not just that he died for the penalty of my sins so I could go to heaven when I died. Instead Jesus preached, "The time has come. . . . The kingdom of God is near.

Repent and believe the good news!" This was uncharted territory for
me, but it was great to finally be on the expedition.

In that short sentence Jesus summarized the gospel, and he
preached on this subject more than any other topic in Scripture: more
than the afterlife, sexuality, morality, marriage, money or religious le-
galism. He spent most of his earthly ministry defining and describing
the kingdom of God. This kingdom was marked by a new kind of people
with a new kind of relationship with God and each other, living out a
new kind of life—one that exuded love for God and neighbor. This love
needed to be expressed through evangelism, world missions, social justice, financial stewardship and vocational calling, among others. The
kingdom of God was meant to heal the planet. To me, this finally felt
like good news, not just for Christians but also for the world.

The splinter was out, but now I had a new problem. While understanding the gospel as "the kingdom of God is near" finally gave me a
theology that could hold all the kingdom values together, it also became
abundantly clear that the current gospel diagrams did not communicate
the fullness of Jesus' statement. We needed something new.

I want to be clear: other diagrams are not incorrect in and of themselves. In the past they have been tremendous tools used by various
ministries to present a clear picture of part of the gospel. At their best
they have rightfully highlighted our need for Jesus to deal with our sins
and to surrender our lives to his leadership. But they have gone wrong
when they became symbols for the whole of the gospel instead of just
a part. At their worst, these illustrations have reduced the gospel to a
system to avoid sin's punishment—here meaning hell—rather than
a way to live the eternal kind of life right now.

Three Movements—

THE DIRECTION OF THE BIG STORY

Thus, to present the central message of our faith in a more complete and attractive way, we need a new summary of the gospel that highlights three movements:

Decision → transformation
Individual → community
Afterlife → mission life

FROM DECISION TO TRANSFORMATION

First, we need a gospel summary that moves away from a one-time decision. In the most distorted version of the gospel message, our irreligious friends are invited to accept what Jesus has already done for them: paying for their sins by dying on the cross. If they accept, they're "saved" by the shedding of Jesus' blood. Dallas Willard puts it more bluntly, calling these converts "vampire Christians who only want a little blood for their sins but nothing more to do with Jesus until heaven."

But Scripture paints a different picture. The Gospel writer Matthew wrote that Jesus came to save us from our sins. The word for "save" in Greek means "to heal" or "to deliver." We're not only saved from the flames of hell, but we have been, are being and will one day be fully healed and delivered from sin itself. Jesus died to free us from the cycles and consequences of sin today and tomorrow, from the sin that lurks deep in our hearts both now and later.

But while we're on the planet, sometimes we feel like we'll crumple into a lifeless heap trying to be like Jesus. He said we would do even greater things than he did, didn't he? But he was, um, *God*. That's a high bar.

Instead of trying, we need to train. As the saying goes, you can walk over the highest mountain one step at a time. That's the idea of spiritual formation—shaping our souls one day at a time. Instead of merely waiting to die for a paradise later, we're called to let God take charge of our lives now. With God's grace we train to become like Jesus and grow in him so we can be his expression of love here and now. We become the kind of good we want to see in the world. Our faith is then real and practical, one that allows us to interact with God on an everyday basis and be changed by his presence. Sure, we still mess up. But for many of us who have no other way to describe our lives except as a living hell, this is welcome news, possibly even good news. Thus, the gospel should include a call to transformation in the present.

I'm not saying that the afterlife isn't important. Of course it is. And it's biblical. Christians, however, must insist that interacting and growing with God in everyday life has the same if not more value. And our gospel needs to compel us to become like Christ, being saved from our sins. In so doing we start to make the shift from an irrelevant, arbitrary truth about the afterlife and make the gospel more relevant to our present world.

FROM INDIVIDUAL TO COMMUNITY

Second, a sense of community is often lost in gospel summaries. They primarily deal with individuals who need to reconcile with God. Though this is indeed true, no one in biblical times would have had the same individualistic view of the self that we do today.

The authors of the Bible assumed they were writing to a community of faith. Though God certainly addressed individuals in Scripture, he almost always did so in a context of community. In the Old Testament, God spoke to leaders and prophets to challenge, correct and encourage the spirituality of the entire Israelite nation. In all cases, biblical characters and their interactions with God were meant as positive or negative examples for the entire community to learn from. In the New Testament, early Christian practice was communal from the outset: believers met often, had intimate relationships, shared resources and worshiped God together. Later, almost every command the apostle Paul would give to a fledgling community of Jesus' followers was addressed to the group as a whole. Texans will like this: almost every "you" in Paul's letters to the churches would more accurately be read as "y'all."

Christian faith is expressed in community—it's not an option. In fact, no faith exists without community. The reflection of the kingdom of God shines through God's people when they're gathered and reconciled. Paul compares Christians to different body parts: though we're different, we all make up one body. We can't be separated or else we're like hands cut off, limp and lifeless. These kinds of images belong only in gruesome horror flicks. And they give me the creeps.

Instead, where two or three are gathered, Jesus is there in the middle of them. And a gospel that highlights community in a culture that longs for intimacy and friendship will feel more relevant to today's culture.

FROM AFTERLIFE TO MISSION LIFE

Lastly, and most glaringly, the afterlife takes priority over the mission life in existing gospel explanations. They imply that the gospel is something that happens after death instead of now. Even if they mention a relationship with God in the present, they often emphasize what people can get out of it—joy, peace, healing, prosperity. As a result, we invite people into a relationship with Jesus without mentioning the *missio Dei,* hoping to get to it later.

Because of this distortion, Christianity has largely focused on what people can get instead of what they can give. And the danger is that we create Christians who are, as Oliver Wendell Holmes put it, "so heavenly minded that they are no earthly good." Our gospel presentations may have allowed people to think they're part of the kingdom without needing to embrace the purpose of loving and blessing others.

But Jesus enticed people into a kingdom mission from the outset. "Come follow me and I will send you out to fish for people." His initial invitation included a selfless call to love and influence others for the sake of the kingdom. And his kingdom is near. We are invited into a space where God is really in charge, where what he wants to happen actually does happen. It's a place of love, joy, peace, patience, kindness, goodness, gentleness, faithfulness and self-control. It's about service and love, not domination and oppression. It's inclusive instead of exclusive, a place for all where our relationships are right, good and healthy. What's more, we can enter into it now, before we die. That's good news—the gospel. As citizens of this kingdom, we're called to spread this kingdom outward.

I was talking with an out-of-town friend about spiritual matters, and he said, "Why do I need Jesus? I'm happy. What else do I need?" He thought Christianity was about what Jesus could do for him, and as he saw it, he was fine. Then God gave me these words: "Your vision of life is too small." I shared an oral version of the diagram illustrated in the story of Caleb, Anna and Shalandra. Since then, he's been more curious about the Christian faith, reading a book I suggested and regularly going to a local church.

As Rick Warren says, it's not about us. By regrafting a missional element into our gospel summary, we can tap into people's God-given dreams to be a source of love, healing and service for others. We need to call everyone into the mission life. And we need to let them know about this call before they become followers of Jesus so they don't get the wrong idea.

To be fair, I'm not saying that these three values—spiritual formation, community and mission—are being ignored in the church. In many vibrant congregations they are embraced and pursued. In fact, theologians from the early church fathers up to the present day have described and articulated the vision of the kingdom of God. These values are ancient and foundational.

Yet our articulation of the gospel in churches and fellowships these days seems to be more about getting into heaven or benefiting personally from Jesus than about joining a healing kingdom movement. What would it look like to communicate the gospel in an entirely different way? How could we connect our presentation of the gospel with answers to the larger questions of life: Why are we here? What's our problem and what's the solution? Where are we going?

The gospel needs to recapture the biblical story—what I call the Big Story. It needs to compete with the larger cultural myths of money, fame, sex and power, which only cause us to be more selfish and self-protective and thus hurt and oppress others with our actions. When sharing the gospel, we need to restore what's good about the Christian message to give hope and healing back to our family, our friends and the world.

Not a Quick Fix —

THE PURPOSE OF THE BIG STORY

Anyone can be an armchair critic. It wouldn't be fair or responsible for me to give my critique and then fail to offer something concrete for others to hold up to the jeweler's light and see if it has clarity, cut and color. So here's my attempt to provide a new gospel summary. With it, I'm trying to do four things.

First, a gospel summary needs to capture a larger scope of the kingdom of God—and make it relevant for everyday life. We need to pull the camera back so we can see the gospel message in the wide panorama of history, culture and the world around us. It needs to break out from the individual level and reach communal and global levels. And it must capture the essentials of Jesus' life, teaching, death and resurrection in the larger context of history and culture. The diagram I've developed with the help of many friends and coministers is not only an attempt to present the core message of the gospel, but also to present the basics of a Christian worldview.

Second, a summary needs to be nestled in the context of the biblical narrative from Genesis to Revelation. People today need to have a sense of drama and story. It's largely where we derive our meaning and purpose. Christians have a wonderful story to tell, and we need to tell it. We have the opportunity to connect personal stories to a larger, more meaningful one.

Third, a gospel summary needs to be simple to understand. Books on the kingdom of God have been around for centuries. But these concepts rarely reach the average believer because they're often vague or complex. To most people these explanations sound like the adults in a Charlie Brown special. How many churchgoers can simply, accurately and meaningfully answer the question, "What is the kingdom of God?" Yet we should be able to. German economist E. F. Schumacher wrote, "Any intelligent fool can make things bigger, more complex, and more violent. It takes a touch of genius—and a lot of courage—to move in the opposite direction."

Though I'm not claiming to be anything close to a genius, I'm hoping that this new diagram will be as simple as possible—but not simpler. My measure of simplicity? It had to fit on a napkin. Until we are able to recommunicate our complex ideas in easy-to-understand ways, we will consistently teach and hear a narrow version of the gospel. We need a simplicity that doesn't avoid complexity, even on the back of a napkin, so that the kingdom can stick meaningfully in the minds and hearts of those who spend most of their time in the cubicle, café or car instead of the church or seminary classroom.

Lastly, the gospel needs to sound like the good news it really is instead of a static message concerned only with the afterlife and thus divorced from everyday realities.

Before I move on, here are four other things you should know. First, the following diagram is not the only way to present the gospel. I'm sure that some upstart in an upcoming generation, as she reads the Bible through a different cultural and sociological lens, will find something suspect in this summary and will create a new one. I just hope it's not in my lifetime. Seriously, I don't claim to have the lock on the truth, and if someone comes up with an illustration that's simpler and more scripturally accurate, then we should go with hers. But this is my best attempt.

Second, feel free to tailor this presentation to your needs. I've provided the framework, but you should choose the paint color, pick the furniture and decorate how you like. If it works better for you to change the order of the presentation to suit your needs, please do so. Use your own stories and illustrations throughout the presentation. This summary is merely the basic flow of the story, and as long as you keep the three levels in mind—systemic, relational and personal—you'll relate the basics of the Big Story well.

My third note is that even though some people may make a decision to follow Jesus through a gospel summary, many won't. Each person will come to faith in his or her own way, led uniquely by God. Diagrams don't save people—the Spirit does. This diagram, therefore, is not meant to be an evangelistic panacea, but a summary to help the presenter understand the biblical story better while also providing a good summary to someone else. Though the biblical narrative has power in and of itself, it is more credible when told through a community of people who live authentically with Jesus, becoming more like him and loving others as he would.

Lastly, though I provide the biblical basis of this diagram along the way, we don't need to share every single Bible verse when presenting it to our friends. I know some of you may find offense with that, but keep in mind that Bono, Oprah and Steve Jobs all have more pull with our irreligious friends than the Bible does. Scripture is obviously more important and authoritative, but even the apostle Paul, who used the Old

Testament generously with his Jewish audiences, was wisely sparing with biblical references in his address to a mix of Jews and Greeks at Mars Hill in Acts 17.

So if your friends ask, feel free to share the biblical basis, but don't inundate them with Scripture references. Pick a select few. If the Bible is not authoritative to them, it'll be boring. More compelling are stories from prevailing culture such as movies, songs, books, blogs, magazines, music videos and the news. Many of these stories tell the truth. But most compelling is your own personal story—and how it connects with the Big Story.

A Walk-Through —

EXPLAINING THE BIG STORY

In each stage of the diagram, it's best to consistently explain how the gospel applies on three levels: systemic, relational and personal. By systemic, I mean the prevailing cultural, historical, political, Institutional and sociological forces that influence our everyday lives, such as racism, sexism and oppression. Think big and global. Relational refers to dynamics between individuals, while personal refers to an individual's physical, emotional and spiritual spheres—anything that relates to his or her relationship with God. Keeping these three levels in mind should keep the diagram from being overly individualistic.

The overall tone of the presentation should feel like a conversation. Ask questions, listen and interact with people's responses. Don't memorize a script. I've provided a lot of detail so you can understand what each part of the diagram represents. But you don't have to share it all with your friends. Just make sure you get the main points and understand the overall flow.

I've also included examples of what I might say along the way, in quotes. My words could change depending on who I'm talking to and our particular situation—I'm not a fan of canned presentations—and yours should too. Feel free to use your own stories or analogies to make it personal. Relax and have fun as you prayerfully share with your friends.

The presentation consists of an introduction, four parts and a response.

INTRODUCTION: ACHING FOR A BETTER WORLD

I decided to start the gospel summary at a place that would connect with my listeners' experience—their ache for a better world. When I first began sharing this diagram, I started with creation, as the Bible does. However, I found that the creation story seemed like a myth or fable to many of my friends. Starting with people's ache for a better world builds credibility that allows me to then go back and present a biblical worldview involving creation and the way the world was designed.

I first draw a circle representing the world in the upper right-hand corner, and a couple of stick figures set slightly apart:

Then I ask, "What's our world like? What do you see on the news?"

Some people may answer that the world is fine (especially Westerners), but I remind them to tell me what's on the news. Most people will then agree that our world is in bad shape, recalling headlines of suffering, violence and oppression. I then draw a squiggly line on the circle, like the ones you find in comic books, to represent damage or shock:

"The world's messed up; that's obvious. But what's more interesting is our response. How do you feel about this kind of world?"

Most people will say that they feel sad or angry or they don't care. A few may say they love it. Listen and interact with each answer.

I'll usually say something like, "No normal person thinks suffering, violence and oppression are good things. All of us long and ache for a better world. And our universal ache speaks of something more. Just like hunger points to food and thirst points to water, so our ache for a better world means that a better world either once existed or will one day exist."

DESIGNED FOR GOOD

Next I draw an outer circle in the top left corner representing the world without squiggly lines because it's a world without damage. Then I draw two stick figures that represent people like us—not necessarily Adam and Eve. They're closer together than the other stick figures to connote community and intimacy. (Note: don't draw the inner circle yet—that comes later.)

"In the Christian worldview, God created a good, wonderful world. In the beginning, everything was right with everything else."

I often use the phrase "in the Christian worldview" when I say

Designed for good

something that people might not readily accept. It gives my listeners permission to disagree with the paradigm instead of reacting personally against me.

Then, I explain this good creation in three parts: systemic, relational and personal.

Design for the world. To keep this simple, I usually only highlight the environment. "On a bigger level, creation was designed to take care of us, and we were designed to take care of creation. We were made to be interdependent on each other" (Genesis 1:29; 2:25). If I have time, I might bring up gender: "And men and women together reflect the image of God—they weren't designed to fight or oppress each other" (Genesis 1:27). If not these, pick a world issue that both you and your listener care about.

Design for each other. "On a relational level, people were designed to take care of each other. They were made to be in true community, with the freedom to love and be loved, to serve and be served, to be themselves without shame in front of each other" (Genesis 2:25).

Design for our relationship with God. "Lastly, on a personal level, we were each designed to be in a relationship with God, one full of love and intimacy. God hung out with us, and we liked being with him. We were meant to love and bless each other as well" (Genesis 3:9). Then I draw the inner circle, which represents the presence of God, where the good things that God wants to happen actually happen and where our personal relationship with God is intact and healthy.

I sum up by saying, "The world and all that was in it was designed for good," and I write, "Designed for good" at the top of the circle.

"But what happened to this good world? How did we get to where we are today?"

DAMAGED BY EVIL

Next, in the upper right-hand circle I draw arrows pointing inward. The arrows represent self-centeredness.

"When God was in charge, we had a wonderful world. But we wanted to be in charge so that all of it—creation and everyone in it—could be used for our own benefit instead of the intended design and purpose of serving each other. It became all about us."

I go through the three levels again:

Damaging the world. "On a bigger level, we damaged creation. We're part of a system that drains the planet for its oil and fills the air with pollutants so we can have a comfortable lifestyle. And the planet fights back in hurricanes and tsunamis. But there are also issues such as racism, sexism, slavery, corruption, injustice and oppression that damage us and our world" (Genesis 3:14-19; Ezekiel 16:49; Amos 5:4-15; Ephesians 6:12).

Damaging each other. "On a relational level, we damage each other and others hurt us—whether we mean to or not. When we live for ourselves, it's easy to take and gain without regard for other people" (Genesis 3:12-13; Romans 1:18-32). Then I draw a squiggly line right down the middle, splitting the people from each other.

Damaging our relationship with God. "And on a personal level, we damage our soul and its relationship with God. We're afraid of God now, and in our fear we try to ignore him and live for ourselves. Therefore we work against God's designs. But we only hurt ourselves, and we will never by the kind of people we want and dream to be" (Genesis 3:10; Romans 1:18-32). Then I draw the inner circle, and then a squiggly line around the inner circle to represent shock and damage to our relationship with God.

"We—and the world—are damaged by evil. We're all contributing to the mess." I write the words "Damaged by evil" over this part of the diagram.

"Where have you seen damage in your own life or the lives around you?"

RESTORED FOR BETTER

"But God loves the world too much to leave it that way."

In the bottom right I draw an outer circle with squiggly lines, representing the larger world that's still damaged. I draw an arrow pointing downward from above, representing God entering into the center of our world's mess by moving into the neighborhood. I also draw a cross that represents Jesus, the king of the kingdom of God.

"God came to the planet as Jesus two thousand years ago and started something new. He started a resistance movement against evil, though not with military revolt or communal escapism. Instead, he taught us a better way to live, and he gives us the power to overcome evil in us and around us."

Designed for good

Damaged by evil

Restored for better

"Ultimately, Jesus comes into the center of our damage, our disease. He gets infected and dies on the cross. But he comes back to life, overcoming the disease, and he offers his immunity to us. In Jesus, we can overcome the selfishness and damage in us and in our world. He has given us the antidote. In so doing, we're all restored for better."

Restoring the world. "On a bigger level, God restored creation so it could be used in good ways. All of the world's systems—the environment, corporations, government, schools—can now be used to usher in his values of love, peace and justice. Oppression and injustice can cease" (Ephesians 2:11-22; Colossians 1:15-20).

If I have time, I might add, "Racism, sexism, ageism and classism have died with Christ and a new way of dealing with people arises. Our exploitation of the planet's resources dies with Christ, and a new way of dealing with the planet arises. This is a new thing, a new world government, where the values are love, justice and peace instead of unfair competition, oppression and violence."

Restoring each other. "God also restored our relationships so we can love and forgive each other. Damaged relationships can be healed" (Matthew 6:12; 18:21-35). I might add, "All enmity and strife between individuals can cease, having died with Christ. We can extend forgiveness to each other, knowing that Jesus has forgiven us for the ways we've hurt each other and, ultimately, him." Then I draw people at the foot of the cross who are learning to become like Jesus.

Restoring our relationship with God. "Lastly, God restored our relationships with himself. People don't have to live self-centered lives or be afraid of God anymore—we don't have to work against his design. Instead we can have a relationship with God full of love and intimacy" (2 Corinthians 5:11-21; Colossians 3:1-17). I might add, "As much as we needed a revolution in the real world, even more we need a revolution in our hearts. We can be reconciled to God. We can have a relationship with him, and our lives can align with his purpose. The old self dies with Christ and the new self rises with Christ. Jesus dies the death we were already dying to give us the life we could not live on our own. We start to live as Jesus did, letting him take charge."

I draw an inner circle that represents the kingdom of God, where what God wants to happen actually happens, like the Garden of Eden in the upper left-hand inner circle. The inner circle's squiggly line is gone, representing a restored relationship with God.

I write the words "Restored for better" on top of this circle. It highlights that God is on a reclamation project, turning the toxic into something useable and livable. The revolution has started to restore a world where evil ran around unchecked, changing what was toxic into something beautiful. One day, this revolution will be complete.

"The good news is that the revolution has begun, and we're all invited. Jesus came to restore the world and everything in it for better."

SENT TOGETHER TO HEAL

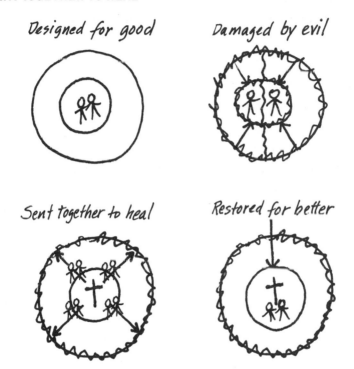

Designed for good

Damaged by evil

Sent together to heal

Restored for better

I then draw the outer circle, which represents the world, and it's still jagged because the world is still in disrepair and we have a lot to do. I also draw the cross, representing Jesus, which is still at the center.

"Jesus wants us to join this resistance movement against evil, to go out and heal the planet."

A word of caution: It's tempting here to focus solely on the kingdom's restoration in the end of time, when all systems, relationships and individuals are made right and good. It makes for good theology: creation, fall, redemption and consummation. But when I shared that with my irreligious friends, it sounded utopian, sterile and boring, like a bad sci-fi movie. Instead, focus on the process of the mission, the fight to heal the planet. Emphasize the adventure and joy of doing something good with our lives. The tension between the now and the not yet is a compelling piece of our gospel that carries the ring of truth.

In this section, I like to reverse the order of the three levels, moving from personal to the relational and ending with the systemic.

Healing our relationship with God. "On a personal level, we're called to submit to Jesus' leadership and become more like him. We need to become the kind of good we want to see in the world. So we admit our contribution to the damage on the planet, and we let Jesus take charge of our lives, we put our trust in him" (Romans 6:23; 2 Corinthians 5:17; Colossians 3:1-17; 1 John 1:9). I might add, "Jesus' leading helps us become more loving, joyful, peaceful, patient, kind, good, gentle, faithful and self-controlled (Galatians 5:22-23). He also leads us into loving others; we are invited not only to heal the world, but to find healing in our everyday lives, to be transformed so we can transform the world." Then I draw an inner circle to represent the kingdom of God and God's presence.

Healing each other. "As we're becoming more like Jesus, we're also called to heal relationships, our own and others. We ask for forgiveness and forgive others. Then we're freed to love each other" (Matthew 6:12; 18:21-35; 2 Corinthians 5:11-21). I draw the four pairs of people near the inner circle.

Healing the world. "Lastly, on a bigger level, we're called to heal systems. One day this healing will be made complete. In the meantime, we're called to protect and heal the environment. We're called to fight injustice and oppression. It's overwhelming, but we're called to do it together" (Genesis 2:15; Exodus 23:1-13; Leviticus 19:9-15; 23:22; 25:1-54; Deuteronomy 15:1-18; Ezekiel 16:49; etc.). Then I draw arrows leading outward, representing God's Spirit.

"Many Christians have gotten stuck in the third circle, not helping to heal the planet. But Jesus wanted his followers to be in this fourth circle, being sent together to heal. In this way, we live out our true design" (Matthew 5:13-16; Luke 9:1-6; 10:1-24; John 17:20-26; 1 Corinthians 12-14).

Then I write, "Sent together to heal" at the top of the circle.

"We don't go alone but with the power of God's Spirit and the community of God's people with us. With these resources, Jesus is asking us to go heal the planet" (Matthew 28:19-20; John 14-16; Acts 2).

RESPONSE

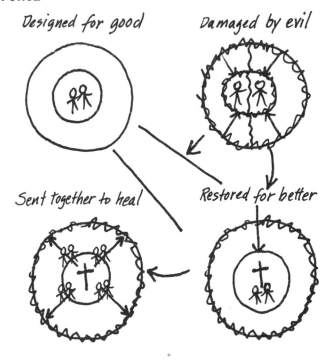

Next, I draw two lines that act as barriers between the "damage" circle and the "healing" circle. I draw one arrow blocked by the barrier, representing our inability to be agents of healing on our own. We'll never make it across the gap by ourselves. Then I draw two more arrows highlighting the path to the fourth circle, which is only through Jesus.

"We can't go straight to the last circle. We need to become the kind of good we want to see in the world. In everything we do, we bring everything we are to it—our motivations, our instincts, our methods. We are all damaged, and we need healing before we can do true healing around us. Jesus does that best. By trusting him and letting him take charge, we can become the kind of good we want to see around us."

If I have time, I might add, "It's easy to be overwhelmed by all the problems in the world, and because we are powerless by ourselves we tend to relate to the world through anger, fear or apathy. Either we fight (which makes others fight back), shrink back, or we don't care. We cannot heal on our own without imperiling our own soul. We need someone infinitely more powerful to rely on, whether we're fighting something out there or something in our own hearts. Jesus, more than any other figure or religion, is on the move to make this world a better place."

I continue, "So, which one of these worlds do you relate to? In the first, everything's fine. Second, you're overwhelmed by the world's or personal problems. In the third, you've made some commitment to Jesus but are holding back. Fourth, you're on the mission of God with his people, but haven't figured out how God fits into the picture. Where are you?"

If they say the first world: "But we already said that the world needs help. What's your role in helping to heal the planet?"

If they say the second world: "Tell me about it. Jesus is offering you a way to overcome it."

If they say the third world: "That's a great start. But it's clear that Jesus is asking you for more. What's keeping you from joining his movement to heal the planet?"

If they say the fourth world: "That's great. What you're doing is in line with the values of the kingdom of God. But you could be doing so much more with God's presence and with his people. You could be a part of something that will last."

Sometimes I add, if I feel like I need to give a longer response, "Think about every major beneficial social revolution in the past two thousand years: public education, health care, human rights, children's rights, women's suffrage, civil rights, literacy education, rights for the disabled, even fair-trade coffee—these and more were all started by Christians. The only major movements I can think of that didn't have Christian beginnings are the nonviolent resistance movements that marked their beginnings with Gandhi. But he learned from the Gospels of Jesus! The followers of Jesus have a good track record of leaving behind the kind of good that lasts."

It's important to acknowledge our failings. "To be fair, there were the Inquisitions, the Crusades and Western imperialism. Yes, absolute atrocities have been committed in Jesus' name and I'm not making any excuses for them. But think of the major irreligious movements of our time. Communism alone claimed one hundred million lives, far more than the Inquisitions and the Crusades combined. I'm just trying to balance things out."

At some point I ask, "Jesus is inviting you to life and join his healing movement for the planet. Will you trust him and allow him to take charge of your life?"

If they agree, I ask them to pray with me: "Jesus, I have been chasing my own dreams and living for myself. It's not only hurt my own soul but others. Please forgive me. I now give you leadership of my life, Jesus. I trust you and want to be aligned with your purposes. Help me be an agent of healing for the world, with your people. In Jesus' name we pray. Amen."

They I say, "Welcome to Jesus' community! You're now a part of Jesus' family. You're forgiven, and Jesus now wants to live in you. Jesus wants you to have the resources for this mission. Would you like to receive his Holy Spirit?" Then I place my hands on them and pray for the Holy Spirit to show his reality and presence in their lives.

Afterward, I might invite them to some next steps.

Join his mission. "What's your part? What is God asking you to do next? This could be anything from starting to recycle to volunteering at a soup kitchen, getting involved with the One Campaign or World Vision, giving your money away to someone who needs it, explaining the faith to someone else. It's ultimately a call to seek the good of someone else instead of yourself. Ask other Christians for good advice on what to do next without burning yourself out. Then act and seek to love people in Jesus' name."

Join his community. "Look for a group of believers who know you and can support you, something like a small group at a church or a campus fellowship. Find a church to plug into. Though faith is personal, it's never just personal."

Join his life. "You are now on the journey to become more like Jesus. Let him take charge of your life. Trust him. Ask for forgiveness for the ways you have not lived out his design. Start to understand how Jesus wants us to live. How does he want you to act more like him? Talk to him through prayer and get to know him through the study of the Bible. Do what he asks you to do."

Again, you'll have to tweak this response so that it's consistent with who you are. But I hope this presentation feels like good news—both to the presenter and its recipient.

Sharing the Big Story —

The campus ministry I'm a part of has been field-testing this diagram with college students and other friends. After hearing this message, some people have decided to start following Jesus. In one example, Jen had been discussing Jesus with her friend Robin through Bible studies. They had met three times already, and on this particular occasion, Jen shared the Big Story on a piece of paper. Through the diagram, Robin realized her greater purpose, and it clicked for her. "I definitely want to join this mission," she said, and she gave her life to Jesus. She asked to keep the paper because she wanted to share the message with her family and friends. And before she moved to another city, she had joined a local church's small group.

One of my favorite stories about the diagram comes from a student named Tyler. He'd met Mike, a self-proclaimed "atheist," at a social justice event hosted jointly by InterVarsity Christian Fellowship and the justice organizations on campus. A few days later Tyler was out on campus striking up conversations about spirituality, and he saw Mike walk by. Tyler stopped him and asked if he could share the diagram with him. Afterward Mike exclaimed, "I thought God would be like that!" His words betrayed his own belief system, and Jesus' message actually sounded like good news to him. Mike and Tyler are still in touch, and Mike has participated in a few Bible studies and our campuswide outreach event. The diagram, in part, helped turn an atheist into a seeker.

A friend of mine, Ryan, is an amazing evangelist and campus staff worker. He's used the Big Story throughout his ministry and has had some interesting results with self-proclaimed Christians as well. With one particular group, Ryan had a hunch that they'd grown up in the church but hadn't taken their spiritual life seriously since coming to college. Ryan shared the diagram with one young man and asked him where he felt like he was. The student evaluated his life right on the spot. He said, "I guess I'm in the third circle but not in the fourth." Conviction set in and he wrestled with not being on the mission of God. So Ryan challenged him further: "What keeps you from being a part of this mission?" He was thankful for the diagram. It not only challenged irreligious people but was a great tool for helping nominal Christians see their role in the wider world.

The last story comes from the other side of the world. I spent a summer in Bangkok working as a consultant to an international church-planting ministry among the world's poorest. My friend Dave lives in Permsup—a slum community built on stilts over a cesspool. I got to know his neighbors, strumming an out-of-tune guitar with drug dealers or worshiping in Dave's home with traditional Isaan tunes while the garbage fumes wafted up between the slats in the floor. I loved being with his neighbors. And when Dave asked me to share this gospel diagram with the house church leaders of various slum communities, I jumped at the chance.

Fifteen indigenous house church leaders from five slum communities gathered together at the ministry's headquarters. I'd been translated before, but I'd never been in part of an interpreted discussion. And the conversation had to be translated into three different languages: Thai, Isaan and English. The conversation was lively, and I presented the Big Story without disclaimers. I just shared the diagram as a summary of the gospel.

The team leader asked a simple question: "What do you think about this?" At first there was silence. My face didn't betray my inner anxiety: had this illustration spoken to them? I had created the diagram with American college students in mind. Would the poor in slum communities find value in it?

But then one older Thai woman spoke up. "I like this. I don't have to make my friends feel like sinners to share the gospel with them. This is something I can share with my neighbors."

Another leader then chimed in, "Yes, this feels like good news to me."

Then a younger male leader added, "This isn't just good news for me. It sounds like good news for the world."

I couldn't believe my ears, and my eyes misted. This diagram contained biblical truth about Jesus' central message, and it sounded good to them too. It freed them to share the message with their neighbors as well. And I felt an urgency to get this message out to as many people as possible. It's Jesus' message, and it needs to be shared.

The Big Story is something you can share with your friends. But it also seems to be releasing Christians to do what they were meant to do, to share the good news. It finally feels like good news, and we've seen people who weren't necessarily "evangelistic" get excited about this message and start sharing it with their friends. My hope is that through learning of this good news, a follower of Jesus will be more willing to share his or her faith with anyone and that irreligious people will be more likely to trust Jesus and his rediscovered message and mission to heal the planet.

So, go out there and share this. Seek to bless your friends with the good news that Jesus came to bring. And may his Spirit be with you, wherever you go.

ACKNOWLEDGMENTS

This book has been a community effort. Many of the ideas were explored and tested by a team of dedicated campus ministers and student leaders who sought to share the Christian message with as many students as possible. Without the passion of the San Diego InterVarsity staff team for the kingdom of God, this book would never have been written. In gratitude, half of the royalties will be given back to the ministries of InterVarsity in San Diego. I'm also thankful to our ministry's prayer and financial supporters, whose partnership releases us into our calling to bear fruit for the kingdom.

I'm also indebted to Dallas Willard, who not only helped me see more clearly what Jesus taught as the gospel, but also encouraged me to write. Don Everts, Sarah Holine, Chris Wheatley, Lars Almquist, Isaac Pollock, Mark Roh, Gerald Choung, Ralph Veenstra, Doug Schaupp, Jamie Wilson and Chris Baron gave me detailed feedback and much-needed cheerleading in the early stages of the book. Ryan Pfeiffer, Andy Bilhorn, Tyler Allred, Kate Vosberg, Terry Erickson, Brian McLaren and Rick Warren offered helpful contributions to the Big Story diagram. I'm thankful to them all.

As for the final product, Al Hsu has been both invaluable and fun to work with: how many editors can give excellent editorial feedback while teasing mercilessly about my mistakes at the same time? And the crew at InterVarsity Press covered all of the details to get this book's message out, and I'm grateful for their professionalism and enthusiasm.

My parents get the credit for passing on their authentic faith to me. And lastly, none of this would be possible without my wife, colaborer and best friend, Jinhee. She has always challenged me to think more clearly—especially on this manuscript—and has offered tremendous support, encouragement and laughter to continue on the journey. As it says in Proverbs 31, many women do noble things, but you surpass them all.

Notes—

Prologue: A Crisis of Faith

page 21   "Do the work of an evangelist": 2 Timothy 4:5.

page 29   "For the wages of sin is death": Romans 6:23.

page 30   Mercy triumphs over judgment: James 2:13.

page 30   No condemnation: Romans 8:1.

page 31   He was saved not by works: Ephesians 2:8-9.

page 32   "Let justice roll on like a river": Amos 5:24.

page 32   Jesus' story of the sheep and the goats: Matthew 25:31-46.

Part One: Designed for Good

page 45   "We're saved by grace": Ephesians 2:8-9.

page 51   "Not bad for a *yuj*": Korean Americans sometimes use this short-
           ening of the Korean word *yuh-ja*, or "woman," as a slang term.

page 54   "We've got more evidence": For further reading, check out Lee
           Strobel's book *The Case For Christ* (Grand Rapids: Zondervan,
           1998).

page 58   "We all ache—groan": Romans 8:19-25 talks about all creation
           "groaning" for its full redemption.

page 62   "In another creation story": In the Babylonian creation myth
           Enuma Elish, Marduk, the god of order, justice and light, kills
           Tiamat, the serpent-goddess of chaos and darkness. Marduk then
           uses Tiamat's corpse to create the heavens and the earth. Frag-
           ments of this epic can be read in James Bennett Pritchard, ed.,
           Ancient Near Eastern Texts Relating to the Old Testament, 3rd

ed., with supplement ed. by James Bennett Pritchard (Princeton, N.J.: Princeton University Press, 1969), pp. 60-71.

page 65   "It wasn't made to fend off lions": Tim Keller used this watch-lion illustration in a sermon at Redeemer Presbyterian Church in New York City on May 31, 1998.

page 65   "In Hebrew, the word *helper*": R. David Freedman, "Woman, a Power Equal to a Man," *Biblical Archaeology Review* 9 (1983): 56-58.

page 66   "It's only after the Fall": In the culture of Moses' time in the second millennium B.C., only a more powerful ruler had the right to rename someone, usually a weaker vassal. Thus, Adam's right to name the animals (Genesis 2:20) was evidence that he was in charge of all creation. Adam merely calls the female a woman in Genesis 2:23, but after the Fall, he names her Eve (Genesis 3:20).

page 66   "Her desire turned toward her husband": Genesis 3:16.

Part Two: Damaged by Evil

page 81   "The World Bank forced India": Vandana Shiva, "The Suicide Economy of Corporate Globalization," April 5, 2004, Counter-currents.org <www.countercurrents.org/glo-shiva050404.htm>.

page 81   "Injustice anywhere": Martin Luther King Jr., "Letter from a Birmingham Jail," in *A Testament of Hope,* ed. James M. Washington (San Francisco: HarperSanFrancisco, 1986), p. 290.

page 93   "The woman you put here": Genesis 3:12.

page 94   "Adah means 'ornament'": Edgar C. S. Gibson, "Some Names in Genesis," in *The Expositor,* ed. Samuel Cox (London: Hodder and Stoughton, 1873), 4:354.

page 95   A cogent argument against polygamy: According to Gordon Hugenberger, the majority of marriages in the Ancient Near East were monogamous; only royalty had numerous wives. In Genesis 1—12, therefore, the author is painting the portrait of two royal lines: the line of God and the line of man. The first instance of polygamy happens in the line of men, with Lamech, who's clearly not a role model. Even in the line of God, the patriarchs and kings with more than one wife are portrayed with great familial dysfunction: Abraham, Sarah and Hagar; Jacob and his wives, concubines and children; David and his family; Solomon and his harem leading him away from God; and so on. It seems that the trajectory of Scripture points to monogamy, with Paul finally saying that Christian leaders should only have one spouse (1 Timothy 3:2, 12; Titus 1:6).

page 96   "people were afraid of God": Genesis 3:8.

page 100   "And in Genesis 10": Genesis 10:4, 20, 31. Actually, the relationship between Genesis 10 and 11 is unclear. It may be an example of paneling, an Ancient Near Eastern storytelling technique in which the narrative isn't recounted chronologically. Instead it is paneled—the same story is repeated from different angles for emphasis. Whether chronological or not, the order of the narrative is important to the Genesis author, who seems to be making a point that the spread of clans and languages is in line with God's "cultural mandate" to "be fruitful and increase in number; fill the earth and subdue it" (Genesis 1:28).

page 100   "Neither male nor female": Galatians 3:28.

page 101   "Uriah the Hittite and Cornelius the Italian": 2 Samuel 11:3; Acts 10:1.

page 102   "Ministers of reconciliation": 2 Corinthians 5.

page 103   "We cannot worship": Matthew 6:24; Luke 16:13.

page 103   "Income of American evangelicals": "Key Trends in Christian Stewardship and Philanthropy," Generousgiving.org <www .generousgiving.org/page.asp?sec=4&page=504#Q2>, World Bank, World Bank Development Indicators. In 2000, the income of American evangelicals was $2.66 trillion, while for comparison's sake, the GDP of Japan was $4.75 trillion, and of the U.S. was $9.76 trillion.

page 103   "One-fifth of that amount": Jorn Madslien, "Debt relief hopes bring out the critics," June 29, 2005, BBC News <news.bbc.co.uk/1/hi/business/4619189.stm>.

page 104   "Our constant need for more": For further reading on wealth and faith, see Richard Foster, *Money, Sex & Power: The Challenge of the Disciplined Life* (San Francisco: Harper & Row, 1985); Ronald Sider, *Rich Christians in an Age of Hunger* (Nashville: Thomas Nelson, 2005); and Kevin Blue, *Practical Justice* (Downers Grove, Ill.: InterVarsity Press, 2006).

page 109   *"Gah-leh?":* Informal Korean for "Want to go?"

page 114   "Or MEChA": MEChA stands for *Movimiento Estudiantil Chicano de Aztlán*, or Chicano Student Movement of Aztlán.

page 114   *Galbi:* Korean barbecue.

Part Three: Restored for Better

page 124   "Moved into the neighborhood": John 1:14 *The Message.*

page 124   "The Sermon on the Mount": Matthew 5—7.

page 126   "More famous rabbis came out of Galilee": "Rabbi and Talmidim," Follow the Rabbi <www.followtherabbi.com/Brix?pageID =2753>.

page 127   "For Jesus, the gospel is": The phrase "the good news of the kingdom" is used two other times: in Matthew 4:23 and 9:35. The phrase "the good news of the kingdom of God" is used three more times, in Luke 4:43; 8:1 and 16:16.

page 127   "Jesus co-opted a military term": Brian Walsh and Sylvia Keesmaat, *Colossians Remixed: Subverting the Empire* (Downers Grove, Ill.: InterVarsity Press, 2004), p. 75.

page 130   "The eternal kind of life": S. H. Travis, "Eschatology," in *New Dictionary of Theology,* ed. Sinclair B. Ferguson et al. (Downers Grove, Ill.: InterVarsity Pess, 1988), pp. 228-31.

page 131   "We usher in heaven": Read *The Divine Conspiracy* (San Francisco: HarperSanFrancisco, 1998) by Dallas Willard for a fuller discussion.

page 132   "Where heaven intersected earth": N. T. Wright, *Simply Christian* (San Francisco: HarperSanFrancisco, 2006), pp. 63-66.

page 132   "The kingdom of God": Matthew 18:20.

page 134   "We are united with Christ": Romans 6:5; Philippians 2:1.

page 134   "Our old selves": Romans 6:8; Colossians 2:20; Galatians 2:20.

page 134   "Our new selves": Romans 6:8; Ephesians 2:5; Colossians 3:1.

page 134   "Pick up our crosses": Matthew 16:24; Mark 8:34; Luke 9:23.

page 134   "To eat his body": John 6:53-60.

page 135   Various interpretations: To learn more about atonement theo-
            ries, see John Stott, *The Cross of Christ,* 20th anniversary ed.
            (Downers Grove, Ill.: InterVarsity Press, 2006) and Brian
            McLaren's *The Story We Find Ourselves In* (San Francisco:
            Jossey-Bass, 2003).

page 136   "The word for 'repent'": Robert N. Wilkin, "New Testament Re-
            pentance: Lexical Considerations," Bible.org <www.bible.org/
            page.asp?page_id=2505>.

page 136   "In A.D. 66": N. T. Wright, *The Challenge of Jesus* (Downers
            Grove, Ill.: InterVarsity Press, 1999), pp. 43-44.

page 136   "The verb means": J. P. Louw and Eugene Albert Nida, *Greek-
            English Lexicon of the New Testament* (New York: United Bible
            Societies, 1989).

page 137   "Seek first the kingdom": Matthew 6:33.

page 137   "The word also refers to justice": I. Howard Marshall et al.,
            eds., *New Bible Dictionary,* 3rd ed. (Downers Grove, Ill.: Inter-
            Varsity Press, 1996).

page 140   "He also saved you *from* your sins": Matthew 1:21. See also
            1 Corinthians 15:3; Galatians 1:4; Hebrews 7:27 and 10:12;
            Romans 5:8; 2 Corinthians 5:21; Galatians 3:13; Ephesians
            5:2; 1 Thessalonians 5:10; Titus 2:14; 1 John 3:16. These pas-
            sages all discuss something more comprehensive than paying the
            penalty of our sins so we can get into heaven.

page 146   "That's way more than Christianity": See Matthew White, "Se-
            lected Death Tolls for Wars, Massacres, and Atrocities before the
            20th Century" <users.erols.com/mwhite28/warstat0.htm>.

page 146   "160,000 Christians die every year": Chuck Colson, "A New
            Century of Martyrs: Anti-Christian Intolerance," June 17, 2002,
            Berean Publishers <www.bereanpublishers.com/Persecution_of
            _Christians/a_new_century_of_martyrs.htm>.

page 146   "Gandhi greatly admired Jesus": Denny Aguiar, "Gandhi vs.
            Christ," September 26, 1992, *Examiner* <www.geocities.com/
            orthopapism/gandhi.html>.

page 147   "We die with Jesus": Romans 6:8; Colossians 2:20; Galatians 2:20.
page 147   "We also live a new life": Romans 6:8; Ephesians 2:5; Colossians 3:1.

Part Four: Sent Together to Heal

page 160   "Come follow me": Matthew 4:19; Mark 1:17.
page 162   "The Christian religion will be judged": A paraphrase of something I remember Dallas Willard saying in June 2004.
page 163   "A cord of three strands": Ecclesiastes 4:12.
page 165   "He promised to be with Isaac": Genesis 26:3; 26:24; 28:15; 31:3; 48:21.
page 165   "When Moses feared the Egyptians": Exodus 3:12; Joshua 1:5.
page 165   "He said the same to Gideon": Judges 6:16.
page 165   "To Solomon and Jehoshaphat": 1 Kings 11:38; 2 Chronicles 20:17.
page 166   "Through Isaiah, God promised": Isaiah 41:10; 43:2, 5.
page 166   "Jesus said to his disciples": Matthew 28:20.
page 166   "The Holy Spirit lives": 1 Corinthians 6:19. This is the only verse that talks about the Holy Spirit inhabiting the temple of an individual. Most other verses speak of the Holy Spirit inhabiting the community of believers, such as Romans 8:9; 1 Corinthians 3:16 and Galatians 3:2.

Epilogue: New Beginnings?

page 185   "What if we brought the tent here": This tent actually exists and is called the "Africa Experience." It was created by World Vision and is available for any campus willing to host it.

The Big Story: Why We Need It

page 191   "In essentials, unity": The quote is often attributed to Augustine, though some scholars disagree. See "A Common Quote from 'Augustine'?" <ccat.sas.upenn.edu/jod/augustine/quote.html>.
page 191   Jesus' prayer for the future Christian community: John 17:20-26.
page 192   Even if the Christian community disagrees: The whole book

of 1 Corinthians deals with issues that were threatening to break up the Corinthian church.

page 193   "What is truth?": John 18:38.

page 193   "The time has come": Mark 1:15.

page 194   This finally felt like good news: Check out Dallas Willard's *The Divine Conspiracy* (New York: HarperOne, 1998) or Allen Wakabayashi's *Kingdom Come* (Downers Grove, Ill.: InterVarsity Press, 2003) for introductions to the kingdom of God.

Three Movements: The Direction of the Big Story

page 196   Vampire Christians: Dalls Willard, *The Divine Conspiracy* (New York: HarperOne, 1998), p. 403.

page 196   Matthew wrote that Jesus came: Matthew 1:21.

page 196   He said we would do: John 14:12.

page 196   Instead of trying: John Ortberg, *The Life You've Always Wanted* (Grand Rapids: Zondervan, 2002), p. 42. Also, 1 Timothy 4:7-8.

page 197   Early Christian practice: Acts 2:42-47.

page 197   Paul compares Christians: 1 Corinthians 12.

page 198   Where two or three are gathered: Matthew 18:20.

page 198   Our gospel presentations: Because of this, I like the direction of recent publications meant for the mass Christian market, such as *The Purpose Driven Life* by Rick Warren. It presents a clear, basic call for the people of God to become more like Jesus and to embrace their God-given purpose to bless others.

page 198   It's a place of love: Galatians 5:22-23.

A Walk-Through: Explaining the Big Story

page 211   Ultimately, Jesus comes into the center: I realize that there are many different angles and theories of atonement that can be explained here. For simplicity's sake, I've chosen one that incorporates the individual, relational and systemic most completely.

page 217   Communism alone: Peter Hammond, "The Greatest Killer," Christianaction.org <www.christianaction.org.za/firearmnews/2004-04_thegreatestkiller.htm>.

ABOUT THE AUTHOR

James Choung is divisional director with InterVarsity Christian Fellowship in greater San Diego. He majored in management science and marketing at MIT, earned his master of divinity at Gordon-Conwell Theological Seminary, and completed his doctor of ministry at Fuller Theological Seminary in postmodern leadership development. In the past, he has served on the pastoral staff of an urban church plant and at a megachurch in Seoul, Korea. He's often invited to speak at churches and conferences throughout the country. He's married and he and his wife have a son.

Choung has also written a companion booklet titled *Based on a True Story* (InterVarsity Press, 2008) and hosts a website called "Tell It Slant" at <www.jameschoung.net>.

LIKEWISE. *Go and do.*

A man comes across an ancient enemy, beaten and left for dead. He lifts the wounded man onto the back of a donkey and takes him to an inn to tend to the man's recovery. Jesus tells this story and instructs those who are listening to "go and do likewise."

Likewise books explore a compassionate, active faith lived out in real time. When we're skeptical about the status quo, Likewise books challenge us to create culture responsibly. When we're confused about who we are and what we're supposed to be doing, Likewise books help us listen for God's voice. When we're discouraged by the troubled world we've inherited, Likewise books encourage us to hold onto hope.

In this life we will face challenges that demand our response. Likewise books face those challenges with us so we can act on faith.

likewisebooks.com